MW00571070

A Hitman Is Cheaper Than Divorce!

How to Stop Dragging That Breakup Ball and Chain

LINDA PENNER

ISBN: 9780995338906 (paperback)
ISBN: 978-0-9953389-1-3 (e-book)
ISBN: 0995338906

For Barb,
a true word wizard.
Thank you for your insightful reviews of these pages
and for giving me your pickle story for chapter 4.
Most of all, thank you for believing in this book.
Rest in peace, dear friend.
I still miss you every day.

CONTENTS

AUTHOR'S NOTE

A Hitman Is Cheaper Than Divorce is a memoir-based work of creative nonfiction. The stories are true, although several characters have been consolidated, and some time frames have been changed to streamline the flow of the story. Most of the names have been changed.

INTRODUCTION

The terrible tangled web we weave through relationship breakdown dates back to the caveman. Grogg bopped his mate over the head with a club, grabbed his curvy little neighbor by the hair, and dragged her off to a new cave. By 1968, it gave Tammy Wynette a number-one hit song and made her as wealthy as the average "D-I-V-O-R-C-E" lawyer. The American Psychological Association states the current divorce rate in North America is nearing 50 percent. This process can make sane people do crazy things to each other, and crazy people do, well…you know.

Divorce was one of the unfunniest things I had ever experienced. But even through all the madness, I clung to occasional shreds of humor that helped me survive with some of my sanity intact. And now, years later, I see women going through many of the same stages that often took me from tears to laughter. Remember, girls, she who laughs, lasts!

1

WEDDING-BELL BLUES

Dear Reader,

If you're reading this, you are probably a friend or relative of mine who has listened to me yak about writing this book for the past twenty years. Or you're someone familiar with the heartbreak, fear, and crap that accompany breakup and divorce. Once upon a time, were you the blushing bride and hopeful romantic? Did you walk down the aisle toward a husband who had everything you were looking for? I did. My man had it all: looks, brains, and a wicked sense of humor. He was the life of the party. He was the king of my castle. I stopped laughing when he became the lyin' king. Then his sense of humor wore thin, and the wicked part began to show through. Did we see the signs of a marriage in trouble?

Red Flags:

- He starts making emergency trips to the supermarket at all hours for Windex or shelf paper.
- He's sporting a brand-new tattoo and test-driving a Corvette.
- You hinted for jewelry or lingerie for Christmas, but he gave you a coffeemaker—the same one he bought his sister for her birthday!
- The classic car he promised you is a 1971 Ford Pinto. (The Pinto had a design flaw that caused it to burst into flames when involved in a rear-end collision.)
- He stops getting his hair cut at old Charlie's place and tries out a new stylist, who gives him blond spikes and introduces him to piercing.
- He gives you a card on Mother's Day that reads, "Across the Miles to You on Your Special Day."

Unholy Matrimony

I had moved along in a fog of feigned bliss through the motions of work, family, and life in the suburbs with our average 2.36 children. (I was pregnant when we moved to the burbs.) My lot was to make sure the household ran smoothly, while my husband presided over our family as his own little fiefdom, dedicated to his ever-changing personal interests. Those interests came with all the trappings of life that money could buy and I could juggle the budget to accommodate. He tired of the company hockey team after one season, and his expensive equipment was put into storage next to the broomball gear, personal gym, fishing rods, crossbow, and a motorbike that hadn't been ridden in years. My backbone had worn thin over the years when it came to standing up to him, regarding the waste of time and money spent on his flights of fancy.

When he signed up for a Wednesday night martial-arts class, I attempted to brace my spine. I told him it was my turn. I wanted to join a dance class on the same evening, and one of us had to be home with the kids. He laughed. Then he told me he worked hard and deserved to have fun and enjoy life. The Novocain I used to numb myself from that logic was to agree that if material things made him happy, we would all be happy. Ladies, it doesn't work that way.

As we became more and more entrenched in our roles from the pages of *Dysfunctional Families for Dummies*, I realized the man I'd married had almost completely disappeared. I tried to pierce his self-centered veneer to find the funny, happy-go-lucky guy I'd fallen in love with. I bought him an expensive tiger eye ring to replace the wedding band he had misplaced. Sexy underwear and weekend getaways did nothing to bring that man back to me. He had disappeared with that gold band.

When I look back, I see that the person Hub had fallen for was gone, too. The feisty, tenacious temptress he had married had become a bootlicking, people-pleasing toady. I had allowed him to mold me into someone else just to keep peace in our home. Someone he didn't want. Someone I didn't want to be.

The Scent of a Woman

In time I began to detect a faint trace that someone else might be benefitting from my husband's positive attributes, which were missing from my life. Hub didn't just run with scissors; he demonstrated some creative behavior that raised a few red flags and got me to start sniffing around for answers to the changes in him. Besides leaving for work early and coming home late, he also began taking the phone into the shower. He started to wear cologne to walk the dog late at night—and he took the car. The last straw came in an envelope with our Visa bill. It showed a recent charge for an expensive dinner at the Red Carpet. A quick glance at the calendar confirmed I hadn't been there to enjoy that meal, since I had been out of town visiting my sister at that time. How dare he take another woman that restaurant? It was the place where we had toasted anniversaries, cheered birthdays, and celebrated the birth of our youngest child. It was *our* place.

That night the Visa bill and I waited silently together for Hub to come home for supper. He was late again. I stirred a pot of leftover stew, while visions of eye of newt, toe of frog, and arsenic danced in my head…joined by anger and suspicion. I was tempted to dump his precious new aftershave into the pot or smash his high-school football trophies or _____ (please feel free to add your own favorites here). I fantasized about shooting him in the head with a huge ball of his own shit but decided to scrub the toilet with his hairbrush instead. There was no sound in the house that evening except the click of my old Bic pen as I drafted Hub's last will and testament.

Shortly after that, a strange and frightening dream began to visit my nights. I was floating in a large lake trying desperately to keep my head above the choppy waves. An ugly, dark, watery hand kept pushing me down, down under while I looked up into an evil tiger's eye.

The Leaving

A counselor's office is a place where you're supposed to be able to bare your soul to a neutral party, in exchange for help with your problems. Hub argued vehemently against the idea. We had tried counseling once before, when I went back to my job after Middle Child was born. It was exhausting to work at the office all day and keep up with the kids as well as the housework. Hub didn't agree with my definition of his share of the workload.

Now, girls, we all know that when your guy actually does something around the house without being told (nagged), he is compelled by some driving force of testosterone to announce it. If Hub ever took the initiative to help out, he would say things like, "I took the garbage out—*for you*" or "I started the dishwasher—*for you*" or "I changed the toilet roll…" Oh wait, that never happened. While Hub tackled a tricky bin liner, I fed the dog, wrote a permission slip for my daughter's school, put a Band-Aid on Peewee's knee, scratched last week's pizza stain off Middle Child's Boy Scout uniform with my nail file while administering a facial spit wash—and made dinner. I remember the time our front porch had been dark for more than two weeks, and when Hub saw me up on a ladder changing the light bulb, he squeezed past me, with the newspaper under his arm, and said, "Why didn't you tell me you wanted that bulb changed? I would have done it—*for you*."

I knew Hub thought cleaning was beneath him, and he couldn't even bring himself to give the bathtub a quick rinse after his coveted morning four-S ritual: shit, shower, shave, and shampoo. I'd had enough—it was payback time! Everyone was still asleep when I crept down to the Halloween trunk in the basement and grabbed one of the old Jackson Five outfits. I pulled a large handful of curly black hair from the wig, tiptoed back up the stairs, and sprinkled them liberally over the bottom of the tub. Then I busied myself making coffee as Hub emerged from the bedroom, scratched his crotch, and stumbled down the hall to the bathroom. He took one look at that tub full of gigantic pubes and unleashed a blaring tirade regarding my poor housekeeping skills. But it worked. He rinsed and wiped the tub—and hung up his towel.

However, Hub's bathtub-cleaning days were soon over. We left the marriage counselor's office with a solution to our problem of sharing chores—we hired a weekly housekeeper. Of course, the cost came out of an already tight budget, so the arrangement didn't last long. I resumed normal household duties—all of them. That round had been an obvious victory for Hub, so I was surprised at how adamant he was against trying counseling again. Then gradually, an ugly suspicion began to jab at the overthinking part of my brain. Perhaps this time he wasn't interested in a solution to our discord. He was looking for dissolution.

A six-foot, two-hundred-pound man can really dig his heels in, when you're trying to get him through the front door of a marriage counselor. Upon our arrival, I immediately apologized to the therapist for the drag marks on his floor. Unfortunately, he met my poor attempt to lighten the mood with a stone face that could rival anything found on Easter Island. The gold band turned around and around on my finger, while I poured my heart out, and Hub sat in silent boredom throughout the entire hour. I'm not sure what I expected from the session—perhaps a blueprint for relationships or some type of Geneva Convention for marriage. I wanted him to grab our marriage by the heels, turn it upside down, and shake the shit out of it. Instead, Mr. Easter-Island-Head sent us home with an assignment on communication therapy. Our instructions were to cut pictures out of magazines and compare our interpretations of the images with each other. By that time, I had so little faith in Hub I wasn't sure he could even use scissors.

We flunked the first test of our homework when we couldn't agree on what magazines to use. I drew the line at *Playboy*, which resulted in a huge fight. Hub claimed it proved we were incompatible and grabbed onto that theory as a life raft to escape from continuing.

"I'm done." He tossed the magazines onto the kitchen floor and walked toward the bedroom.

I followed him down the hallway and mustered a firm, take-charge voice. "Hey, we are *not* done!"

Hub never made eye contact with me as I watched him take a large gray suitcase from the closet and begin emptying his dresser drawers into it.

I drew a jittery little breath and found that my vocal cords had shut down. The take-charge voice was silent. The only sound was a loud snap, when Hub closed the suitcase. Then he mumbled some old clichés about "wanting space" and "needing to find himself." It all came down to wants and needs—his.

My voice rasped. "I hope you realize our kids will be dragged into this wreckage along with us. What are you going to tell them?"

"Me?" It was the first time Hub looked at me since he started packing. "I thought you could do it—you're better at this kind of thing."

The voice firmed. "Kind of *thing*? What kind of thing do you think this is? And what makes you think I'd be better at it than you?"

Hub reached for his case, and I grabbed his wrist.

The voice was steel, "You are *not* walking past those kids with that suitcase and no explanation!"

Hub shook my hand off his arm and turned away from me. "Take them next door to play. We'll tell them next week."

I hurried into the family room and turned off the TV. "I'm going to the Turners' for coffee, and you guys are coming with me. You can ride your scooters on their RV pad."

"Yeah!" the boys shouted and ran to put on their sneakers.

"Mom, I'm too old for that." My daughter pouted. "Can I go to Stop-N-Go for Slurpees?" She struck the familiar hand-on-hip stance and held out an outstretched palm in front of me. I was in no mood to deal with that attitude, so I pulled some money from my stash on the top bookshelf. My hand brushed our family photo, and it toppled to the floor. Glass crunched under my foot as I stepped on all those smiling faces and walked to the door.

Fran Turner put two steaming mugs on the table, and mine sat untouched in front of me. We'd never been friends, and the only thing we had in common was that our boys were the same age. Today we had even less in common—she still had a husband. When I looked at the coffee, my stomach sent up a strong message warning me of mutiny if I drank it. No matter; my hand was too shaky to get the cup to my lips without spilling. Fran was talking, but I couldn't hear anything except a strange pulsing in my head.

I didn't dare speak. *Shut up, shut up, shut the fuck up!*

The coffee cup rotated in my hand while I counted and re-counted the tiny blue flowers on the rim. Twelve. I didn't know what time it was, but seeing the clock on her gleaming black stove made me feel I'd been there long enough. Long enough for Hub to have left the house. Left us.

I pushed the blue flowers away, got up from my chair, and went home in a daze, leaving Fran talking and my kids in her backyard.

I needed some time on my own to try to sort out the jumble of emotion chewing up my insides. When I opened the front door, I was shocked to see Hub sitting in his brown leather Father's Day chair. For one tiny moment, I thought he had changed his mind, and then I saw the two suitcases in the hall. The luggage I'd bought for our Hawaiian dream vacation. The dream we canceled to go to Hub's family reunion.

"What the hell are you still doing here?" I asked.

"Waiting to say good-bye to you."

"You said all your good-byes to me long ago—long before you packed those bags. Now get out—*get out!*" I screamed. Tears railed against the corners of my eyes, but I refused to let them out.

I looked down and began to pick jackets and toys up off the floor in a frantic struggle for normalcy. Hub rose from his chair with calculated ease, grabbed the suitcases, and started for the door. His head did a Linda Blair–type swivel around the room with a look tinged of smug satisfaction. When my knees touched the floor, I realized Hub had goaded me into giving him absolution to leave with my final two words...get out. I tightened my grip on the water pistol in my hand and wished it were real.

Hub had always been my rock. When the door slammed, that illusion crumbled to dust. It brought reality down on my shoulders with a sudden and terrifying weight. So began the ongoing burden of divorce that became a new rock in my life: the perpetual rock of Sisyphus.

I ran to the bedroom and closed the door to shut the world out and closed my eyes to shut myself in. Curled up on the bed like a fragile fiddlehead, I had to confront the fact that I'd been running from the truth for a long while—running blind to keep from facing a bad marriage that was snapping at my heels. Well, it finally caught up and bit me in the ass. When I opened my eyes, I was looking at the half-empty closet.

I pushed myself up off the bed and went next door to get the kids.

After we got home from the Turners, part of me sat on the floor in the corner and watched the rest of me prepare dinner, feed the kids, supervise bath time, read a story, start the laundry, pay the paper boy, and unplug the phone. It forced me to believe that Hub was trying to call but couldn't get through.

There was nothing to stop the tears for a long time, but the sandman finally came in the wee hours that first night on my own, and I dropped into a semi sleep. I dreamed the bedroom carpet stretched out the door and into a beautiful green meadow surrounded by dark fringes of forest. I got out of bed and felt the soft grass under my feet as I walked along underneath a bright-blue sky. It was like a peaceful out-of-body experience, and I saw myself tying Hub to a railroad track with the old 5:15 steamer bearing down on him.

I woke still dressed and shivering on top of the bedcovers. The striped slivers of morning light were creeping through the blinds across Hub's side of the bed—the empty side. He was gone, and I was left with a tension headache, a teenager, a ten-year-old, and a toddler. How could he just walk out on us? I would have gone to the ends of the earth for him. I had done it before, a dozen years ago, when we moved to that crazy place in the mountains.

A Tin Town

One evening, in the early days of our marriage, I had just slapped a pan of Hamburger Helper on the stove when Hub rushed in and told me he had quit his job and was heading for the hills. There was money to be made at a new coal-mining development. A few months later, when my head stopped spinning, I quit my job too and followed him. He liked the idea of living in a place where he could advance with a new company. I liked the idea of living in a place where we could afford to buy a house and raise a family.

I remember my first visit to that coal town well. I set off toward the Rockies when the sun was high and bright, and so were my spirits. When I stopped for fuel at the halfway point, I boasted to the old gas jockey that I was on my way to a better life in a new mining community.

"Just a tin town," he said, took my money, and turned away without another word.

Both the sun and my high spirits were gone by the time I arrived at my destination and had a good look around. My first impression was that if the country ever needed an enema, this would be the place to administer it. At the town's edge, the paved highway abruptly turned into streets of muddy sand. Everything was either brand new or half-finished. All the trees had been sheared off the side of a mountain to carve out this community—a forest completely stripped away by the march of progress. My little Datsun slowly crept along street after street lined with skeletons of cookie-cutter houses under construction. All I could see were rocks and dirt, with a few sickly green patches of lawn struggling here and there. The rest of the town was made up of mobile homes, including the town office and a bank. I inched past several trailer parks and a playground without a single tree, blade of grass—or child. Just some lonely swings and a slide in the middle of a pile of gravel. A tin town.

The downtown core had a brand-new school, a combination grocery store and post office, and a modern motor inn. I pulled into the hotel parking lot, rummaged through my purse for a dime, and went in to use the phone. There was Hub, propping up the bar.

"You made it!" He jumped off his stool and grabbed me in a big bear hug. The lopsided grin told me he'd been there awhile.

Smoke filled the dim tavern, and it reeked of stale beer and BO. And something else...the way the carpet smelled when we got our puppy. I remember being surprised to see so many people there during the afternoon. Some were playing pool, some shuffleboard—all drinking. I ordered a beer and tried not to stare at the pornographic ink crawling over the bartender's arms.

"There's a dance here tonight," Hub said and pointed to a garish promotional poster on the wall while signaling for the waitress to bring some menus.

Through the smoky haze, I could see the poster featured a local Bee Gees cover trio, headlining themselves as Three Free Drinks.

"Don't know why these guys always pack the house. They're not that good," Hub mumbled.

"Um...really?"

We choked down our meal without any further conversation. I convinced myself it was because of the loud music from down the hall that signaled the dance was about to start. Hub hurriedly paid the check and told the disinterested, gum-chewing waitress that his steak had been "dry as a popcorn fart."

When we entered the large, dimly lit room, Three Free Drinks were on stage, making a gallant attempt at "Staying Alive," and there was a definite nightclub atmosphere, complete with disco ball. As my gaze scanned over the throng of coalminers, I worried that my new skirt was a little too short. That apprehension evaporated when I spotted a pair of red leather hooker boots topped with a micro mini that made me look like Granny Clampett. That skirt wasn't keeping any secrets—not even Victoria's. The silicone sister standing beside Micro Mini had a hemline invisible to the naked eye. It seemed to be hidden somewhere under a shimmery silver jacket with shoulders designed by George Lucas and buttoned below her exposed navel. She was at least six feet tall in her patent platforms, and since my husband considered himself to be the consummate connoisseur of gams, he felt compelled to point out that "her legs went all the way up to her armpits."

I felt Hub slide a protective arm around me as he introduced a few of his workmates—Shorty, Lefty, and Frenchy. More like Dopey, Grumpy, and Sleazy, I thought and wrestled my fingers from Frenchy's prolonged handshake. He could have generously shared his hair gel with all of his buddies and still had plenty left for that mullet. Lefty had no problem that a good dental plan couldn't fix, and Shorty was...well. The boys were all in best bib and tucker—identical white T-shirts. The Drinks began playing a slow set, and when Shorty got up to dance with the monumental Micro Mini, his head only came up to those sharp points on her chest. I was genuinely afraid he might lose an eye, but judging by the look on his face, he wasn't worried about a thing.

Hub ordered drinks for anyone within shouting distance, and I realized I was the only other woman in the room, aside from the two lovely ladies of the evening. I'm sure business was brisk for them that night in the testosterone-filled room, and the Hustle wasn't just a favorite dance back then.

After that dubious introduction into our new community, I rolled up my sleeves and made the most of it. Hub and I worked hard, bought our first home, and started our family there. By the time we moved back to the city, we had made enough money for a down payment on my dream home in the suburbs. Now, I stood alone in the kitchen of a house that was fast becoming my nightmare. I had always considered Hub the foundation of that house, but he was only one flimsy wall. I had hung onto that wall like a boring picture at a low-rent motel.

2

ANOTHER ONE BITES THE DUST

Dear (insert your name),
Well, he's gone. In the beginning, you probably moved on autopilot and maybe even wondered if there was a chance of reconciliation. Were you drinking a bit more? Had you started to smoke again? Did the volume of your tears encourage people to buy shares in the tissue industry? I was stretched to transparency with worry while attempting to keep it all together in a frightening, hazy numbness. Getting through each day was tough enough when the breakup was still so raw, and then the dreams came to screw up my nights, too. At first I ignored the warning signs that my husband was never coming back.

Red Flags:

- The new TV, barbeque, and the grade-A steaks in the freezer are all gone, but the wedding pictures and the kids are still there.
- When you cancel your appointment with the marriage counselor, he gives you the number for a real estate business he operates as a sideline—in case you have to sell your house. How unprofessional!
- You find yourself thinking that taking out a contract isn't just a term for corporate agreements.
- The seat is always down.

A Hitman Might Be Cheaper

Overnight, my life had turned into an enormous bucket of poo. Each day, I would reach into that bottomless pit and clean off as many things as I could. The next day, I'd start all over again with the same stinking mess. I was an automaton, going through the motions at work as well as taking care of the house, yard, and vehicle. I was getting the kids to school and their activities, doing the shopping, keeping medical appointments, and attempting to balance a much tighter budget. One step forward and two steps back became a new dance for me called the Single-Mother Shuffle.

There was a lot of advice coming at me from people at work about protecting my assets with legal counsel. I balked at that. I felt that taking steps to a law office would be walking away from my marriage. But Hub wasn't paying regular support for the kids, and that was my ultimate push toward finding a lawyer I could afford. I found the cheap ones were sleazy, and some of the expensive ones were both—cheap and sleazy. But they all charged more than I could afford. It reminded me of one of those old lawyer jokes I used to think were funny:

A girl sits down next to a well-dressed man at a bar, gives him an approving glance, and says, "Hi there, handsome. I'd screw you." She looks around the room and continues, "As a matter of fact, I'd screw anybody in this place!" The guy immediately signals for the check, turns to her with a big grin, and says, "Hey, I'm a lawyer, too!"

When my friends found out I was contemplating divorce, they also felt compelled to join my coworkers in the game of who could give the most advice. They seemed to think I didn't have a clue about such matters and acted as though my husband took my brain with him when he left. But these people all agreed on one thing—the best way to survive a divorce was with a good lawyer. After putting the down payment on a retainer to the professional services of Plumb and Associates, I began to think the lead pipe, candlestick, or revolver might be a more affordable way to get out of this marriage.

My soon-to-be-ex-husband was livid when I told him I had started legal proceedings. He wanted to carry on just as we were—living apart but knowing that his family was within reach, if he ever wanted us. I was in marriage limbo, and it made me realize there was nothing left for me to hang on to. My marriage had been a big front, like a carnival cutout board where couples stick their heads through two holes to be transformed into a curvaceous supermodel and a muscular hunk. I was left with just the holes.

Since Hub left, I felt our neighbors in the close-knit community of Perfectville were all watching my every move. The curmudgeonly old bat from across the street had never once looked up at me from under her big gardening hat until the news buzzed down the gossip wire that my husband had moved out. But one day, when I got home from work near the end of that first awful month, there she was, standing at my front door with a big, muddy fistful of radishes. I was shocked to see she had bothered to come down from her usual vantage point under the eaves. Mrs. Bat-Woman quickly stuck her foot in the door, pushed past me, and plopped the dirty mess of wormy vegetables into my kitchen sink. Her periscope neck craned around the kitchen at the unpacked grocery bags on the floor and then snaked down the hall to get a better look at the overflowing basket of laundry, scattered schoolbooks, jackets, and toys.

"Hubby not home for supper, yet?" The sweet, syrupy words dripped from her Cheshire grin and down the front of her flowery muumuu while she pointed a long, dirty fingernail at the pot of Kraft dinner bubbling over onto my stove.

"No, he's out picking up hookers with your husband at that new strip club."

I still hate radishes.

The neighborhood women started avoiding me, and I became the leper of suburbia, wearing a big scarlet letter "D." They were all convinced divorce would make me desperate to pounce on their husbands—guys who were mostly carbon copies of the one who had just walked out on me. Beelzebub from next door hadn't spoken a word to me in five years, except to yell at my dog, but, out of the blue, he phoned to ask me over for a drink, in the middle of the afternoon. He exemplified the perfect hat trick of masculinity. He could open a can of beer with a BBQ fork, scratch his massive hairy back with it, and then use it to flip a steak. He probably even stepped out of the shower to pee.

"Sure, Bubba, I'd love to have a drink at your house. I'll bring my cooking sherry. Unfortunately, I used the last of it in my Christmas baking, so all that's left is in some old fruitcake. Speaking of fruitcake,

I think your wife should be home around four thirty. I'll come over then. Oh, it's no trouble at all...hello...hello?"

Wastin' Away in Perfectville

After a few weeks, stress became my new worst friend, and I knew I had to start eating properly if I was going to survive. My black-coffee diet was mainly supplemented by roughage from my fingernails, and I'd lost so much weight even my underwear didn't fit properly anymore. Laundry day brought its own set of frustrations. I noticed the cheap elastic in my new downsized undies was already torn and stretched to Mama Cass proportions. Commando looked like my only option until payday.

I continued folding clothes from the dryer and began eyeing Middle Child's tighty-whities in a whole new way. My first confession is that his underwear drawer was missing a few Y-fronts that day, and my second is that I replaced them on payday along with several extra pairs for myself. I still find men's underwear is much better quality at a better price, and they come in a variety of shades with some very sexy styles. I guess that would be a third confession.

Going Postal

Within a short time, my frayed nerves were as stretched as the elastic in those discarded panties and finally snapped when I arrived at the post office to find that my mailbox key wouldn't work. I waited impatiently at the customer service counter, while Mary Hard-Faced-Bitch slowly finished sorting a small stack of letters and waddled over to advise me that Hub had removed my name from our postbox. The old silverback bared her lipstick-covered teeth in a false smile and informed me the rental fee on a new box would be seventy-five dollars—in cash. Her wrinkly cleavage wobbled above the counter, and her condescending stage whisper insured everyone in the building witnessed my humiliation. Old Mary was the kind of tight ass we've all heard about who can make dogs howl when she farts. Cocktail hour on a summer's eve with that old bag would probably consist of vinegar-and-water martinis. Her white, fish-belly underarm flapped furiously as she snatched the money from my hand—my grocery money. I picked up my new postal key and what was left of my pride, walked out, and slammed the door—on my finger!

The Great Escape

Each evening, after the kids were in bed, I'd settle down in my big comfy chair with a glass of wine or a wimpy cup of tea, like Chamomile Calmer or Simple Soother, to unwind from the day. I called it my great escape, but in reality I wasn't escaping from anything. I was just feeling sorry for myself, concentrating on all the terrible injustices in my life, real or perceived. On rare occasions, I'd invite one of the old friends from Hub's liquor cabinet, Jim Beam or Johnnie Walker. But there were always tears when those boys joined me.

There is nothing wrong with a little self-indulgent venting, but when you've spit it all out, the bad taste should be gone. You need to move on or implement a plan of action. Rehashing the same things over and over resolves nothing.

Solitary pity parties set the tone for most of my evenings and gradually began to spill over into my daily life. I started to look at my situation through lenses clouded with what-ifs.

What if the Christmas bonus hadn't been canceled this year?
What if I won the lottery?
What if I'd finished college?

What if Hub hadn't left me?

What if I'd stayed single?

I continued to drag out of bed each day and shake off the gloom until one miserable Monday morning. The day care had closed for ant extermination, and I stayed home from work with Peewee. A chance to spend some one-on-one time with him should have been a treat for both of us, but that day I was at an all-time low. Hub refused to pay any further child support until our agreement was hammered out in court, and the stress of my financial situation consumed me.

After confiscating a pantyhose slingshot from Middle Child's backpack, I sent him off to school with his sister. Then I zipped Peewee into his favorite red Spiderman jacket and sent him out to play in the backyard. He loved to play outside in any kind of weather, through rain, sleet, and snow—he would make a good mailman someday. I watched the little red point of his hood bob up and down in the sandbox as he constructed a new freeway with his digging machines. It would be a pajama day for me, so I poured a cup of coffee and escaped to my favorite chair, melting into the comfy blue plush in a big, gooey pile of self-pity.

I don't know how long I sat there and allowed all the same old what-ifs to act out an unrealistic scene on the stage in my mind. Eventually a new, unannounced player crept silently into the spotlight.

What if Peewee had never been born? How much simpler my life would be.

Regret and guilt immediately rushed in and brought the curtain down. I struggled out from under my shameful refuge, knocking the cold coffee to the floor as I ran to the window. No red hoodie. I cleared the back steps in one leap and raced through the yard.

No hoodie—no little boy!

Both gates had safety latches, and the fence was too high for him to climb over. Or was it? I ran next door and punched the Turners' doorbell until Fran opened the door a crack to reveal her poker face. She said she hadn't seen Peewee that morning, and as her beady eyes looked down at me from the lofty height of her roman beak, she told me her son's Big Wheel bike was missing from their carport.

Oh *no!* Peewee loved that shiny red bike, and he'd be able to cover a lot more ground on it than if he was walking. The Turners were likely to press charges of grand theft cycle.

I ran to the park at the end of the street calling, shouting, screaming, and silently praying for a glimpse of that red hoodie. Nothing.

I jogged around the block and back to my house on throbbing feet, wishing I'd taken time to put shoes on and that I hadn't started smoking again. There was no sign of Peewee along the way home. I grabbed my keys from the hook at the back door and jumped in the car. My hands were shaking so hard I could hardly keep them on the wheel as I drove up and down the nearby streets in Pleasantville. After cruising right through a second stop sign, I knew I needed help.

The wait was excruciating and seemed to take hours before the police car arrived in front of my house. I could see the curtains move in Gwen Turner's front window next door as I raced out to meet the police officer. She would have been busy hot-dialing her neighborhood gossip cult, and everyone on the street would know I hadn't cared for my child properly. But no one came out to offer any kind of help.

I can't seem to recall the policeman's name, so I'll refer to him as Smith. I remember he was a take-charge kind of guy and showed no emotion or sympathy toward me. I was glad. I didn't deserve it. He took one look at the haphazard way my car was parked on the curb and insisted I hand over my keys. Then he instructed me to wait at the house in case Peewee found his way back home.

After the officer left, I chewed my nails and wore down the carpet between the window and the phone. I knew I had to call Hub, but I couldn't face him. One glance at my face would tell him it was all my fault, and he'd know what I'd been thinking. The whole world would know that I had thought my life would be easier without my little boy.

I picked up the receiver and began to trace his number with my fingertip, but the phone slid from my hand to the floor. A police cruiser had pulled up, and I could see a Big Wheel in the backseat. My feet hardly touched the grass as I flew across the lawn to meet Constable Smith. He climbed out of the cruiser shaking his head.

"We found the bike, but there's no sign of him."

A low buzz began to fill my head, and the louder it got, the faster the ground came up to meet me. When I opened my eyes, I saw two blurry, blue uniforms hovering above. I thought I was see-ing double, but when the sky finally stopped spinning, I felt two policemen reach down and help me back onto my feet. The second officer introduced himself, but that was when I realized I was still in my pajamas, so I don't remember his name, either. I'll call this one Jones, and he had a partner with him. Three policemen—the cavalry had arrived!

Smith steered me into the kitchen and handed me a glass of water. He explained that the bike had been found stuck in a recent-ly dug trench in front of an apartment building on Eaton Street, about seven blocks from our house.

"Lily!" I sobbed. "My friend lives in that building! How the hell did he get all the way over there? How did he know where—"

A squawk from Smith's radio interrupted my frenzied outburst, and he stepped out onto the front porch to answer. I grabbed the phone off the kitchen wall and dialed Lily's number. It rang on and on into her empty apartment. I knew she'd be at work, and I don't know what I expected to achieve by calling her, but I had to do something.

I still had the phone to my ear when I heard the wail of a siren and saw the flashing lights of a police car coming down the street. In the backseat, I could see the point of a little red hoodie. When I reached the car, I yanked the door open and felt two precious, chubby arms around my neck.

Peewee wriggled against my iron grip and pointed to his uniformed rescuers. "My cops!"

A Three Dressed Up as a Nine

The ongoing battle of survival left me with little time for myself, and the highlight of my new single life was an invitation to a coworker's wedding. The last thing I wanted was to see another grinning couple at the altar, but I had heard it was a Vegas-style ceremony with an open bar. I was in desperate need of a good laugh and a free drink—or two. So I started to think it might be fun to get out on the floor for a few rounds of the chicken dance. The problem of an affordable gift was solved when I unearthed the coffeepot Hub had given me the previous Christmas, instead of the lingerie I had hinted for. The disappointing gift remained unopened in the storage room, and he had never even noticed. Ultimately, it was the thought of being served a nice, all-the-trimmings dinner while sitting at a beautifully decorated table that convinced me. Those days, most of our meals were eaten in the car as I shuttled the kids between soccer games, music lessons, swim meets, and parent-teacher meetings. Chomp, smack, slurp—spill.

The day of the wedding was beautiful, and I had started to look forward to it until I faced the dilemma of what to wear. My wardrobe consisted mainly of corporate or slob clothes. The spiffy, Sunday-go-to-meetin' section was almost sackcloth and ashes. I began to scrutinize the contents of my bedroom closet and storeroom until I felt like Scarlett O'Hara eyeing the drapery. My favorite seafoam-green dress was old, but it was designer quality, and it fit great—thanks to my recent black-coffee-and-fingernail diet. I'd already worn this dress to several corporate functions, and most of the people from my office would be at this wedding, so I wanted to change the look. I took the sash off and used it as a band on my sun hat and then threw on a contrasting pashmina. A quick twirl in front of the mirror confirmed it looked pretty damned good. I needed a swift kick for not buying more good clothes for myself during the halcyon days when Hub and his salary both still lived with me.

Take my advice, girls. If your guy starts talking about "finding himself," clean out the bank account, max out his credit cards, hide the family heirlooms, and, if he has any jewelry—take it. Survival mode kicked in for me as soon as Hub walked out. The first thing I did was buy several cases of canned mushrooms that were on sale. Do not do that. Surviving means *cash*—not canned goods!

A glance at my watch told me it was almost time to leave for the wedding service, so I put dinner on the table—in the form of cash and the number for Fast Pizza. I left the babysitter popping her gum and flicking channels with the kids while I ducked into my bedroom to make the dreaded monthly telephone call.

I shouldn't have made that call.

Hub wasn't voluntarily paying toward the children's upkeep, but I had learned if I called him around payday, he would part with some of his precious cash. He would rarely bring the money to me, and I hated going to his apartment to get it. The last time

I was there, I noticed a new upmarket stereo system with a set of Bose speakers that would make any professional DJ jealous. I had put off calling him all week, but the time had come to surrender my last bit of dignity and beg the father of my children for money. I hoped for voice mail, since I was never sure which of his two personalities would answer. To my surprise he picked up on the first ring, and the amiable Dr. Jekyll was on the line.

"Sure, I'll get the money to you first thing Monday. Too bad the kids aren't here today. We've had lobster flown in for dinner!"

The kids…lobster…WE?

I slammed down the phone, threw my hat across the room, and cried all the way to the church. Trembling legs forced my body to the top of the long, stone steps, and I covered my puffy Kermit the Frog eyes with sunglasses. I couldn't take those shades off for the entire service. I slunk into the back pew and began formulating a plan to go shopping for a pearl-handled derringer after the ceremony, when a parade of six bridesmaids began to distract me. They were outfitted in off-the-shoulder, red-satin, saloon-style can-can dresses, accompanied by the mandatory black fishnet stockings. I began to experience a strange sensation at the back of my throat and realized it was a feeling I hadn't experienced in a while—laughter. I swallowed the tickle and tried to concentrate on my upcoming firearms shopping spree and the location of Hub's life insurance policy. Then came the bride, in a sequined, showgirl-style, off-white gown, complete with gigantic feather headpiece. I squeezed my hand against my throat in a vain attempt to stop the persistent giggle. But when an Elvis impersonator stepped up to the pulpit in his skintight white jumpsuit, I knew the wedding ceremony was over for me. I waited for fake Elvis to break into his resounding rendition of "Burning Love," slipped off my shoes, and tiptoed out.

My first solo social event began with apprehension, then spiraled into misery with a phone call and ended up a wonderful, barefoot, out-of-control laughing fit in the parking lot. The newlyweds didn't fare quite as well. Their Vegas marriage was over before the eight-by-ten glossies were out of the darkroom.

That night, my dream of revenge returned. I was in the middle of Pleasantville in my seafoam-green dress. The street was full of cops riding Big Wheel bikes. Bubba, Bat-Woman, and Mary Hard-Faced-Bitch stood outside the lines of yellow crime-scene tape wrapped around Hub's car. They were holding torches and pointing at me. "Unclean, unclean!"

Where There's Smoke...

In some strange way, that dream seemed to strengthen my resolve. Then, just as I started to hold my head up on the streets of Pleasantville, a new ugly thing began to rear its head. Hub started to miss soccer games, school functions, and time with the kids. We all know that during some marriage breakdowns, there are misguided parents who want their children to choose between them and even balk at shared visitation. That was never an issue in our case. Hub made his own sporadic schedule. I guess he thought the kids might need more fodder for therapy.

When he reneged on his promise to take them on an overnight campout, I jumped to instant damage-control mode. I told them I would take them. On reflection, that wasn't such a brilliant idea, since my definition of roughing it has always been a hotel without room service. I also had no camping equipment, and the thoughts of that dilemma brought me back to the moment that defined the beginning of the end of our marriage.

It had happened the previous year when Hub purchased some state-of-the-art tenting gear for a fishing trip. He came home three days later with the camping equipment still in pristine condition and hotel towels in his suitcase. I had overlooked a great deal of Hub's questionable behavior, but the significance of those towels was not lost on me. In a desperate attempt to purge the thought of his low-rent rendezvous from my mind, I had thrown all the gear in the garbage, along with his fishing tackle and T-shirt that boasted, "I Have a Titanium Rod."

A coworker stepped up to rescue our outdoor adventure and gave me an old tent out of her attic, along with a Coleman lantern. The kids bounced off the walls with excitement as they rolled up the quilts and pillows from their beds. I packed some pop, snacks, and hot dogs and grabbed a roll of toilet paper—just in case.

We hit the road and drove until we found a wooded picnic area. The first order of our trip was to set up the musty-smelling tent. To my delight, it had all four pegs, which Middle Child managed to pound into the ground with a rock and without a single smashed finger. But when I pushed the pole up into the middle of the old tent, it tore through the rotting canvas, and the whole thing came down on my head—spider webs and all.

I was not giving up! We were there to camp—and we were staying overnight!

I knew the only way to overcome the erectile dysfunction of the tent—and get it up—was to plug the gaping hole at the top. After a few failed attempts involving some twigs and a package of Twizzlers, I rolled my jacket into a ball, tied it to the end of the pole by the sleeves, and jammed it into the gap in the canvas. It worked—the pole stayed up! While I was engrossed in completing this amazing feat of engineering, the kids had gathered quite an impressive amount of wood. I'd never built a fire before, and as my stack of burned matches continued to pile up, I finally realized our logs needed help. I sent the boys off on a mission to gather dry leaves and small sticks while my daughter broke out the snacks. As soon as our kindling was strategically placed and finally burning, it started to rain.

I was still not giving up! We were there to camp—and by golly, we were staying overnight!

The four of us piled into the car with our bedrolls and dug into the pop and chips. I was glad the kids had talked me into lugging a big box of comic books along with us at the last minute. We took turns reading to each other, and soon we were making up our own characters and stories. We dubbed ourselves the Incredible MC, Superpants Kid, Miss Artsy-Fartsy, and the Fading Woman. My daughter found my grocery pad and a pen in the hatchback and created some super sketches for our superheroes. We were laughing and having such a good time we hardly noticed the rain had stopped. When most of the snacks were gone, I decided a hike before our wiener-roast supper would give the wood time to dry out. It did not. No matter how hard I tried, I could produce nothing but smoke signals in that fire pit.

I was *not* giving up! We were there to camp—and we were bloody well staying overnight!

We needed dry kindling. By this time, I had started to think like a woodsman (woman), so there was only one solution. The comics would have to be sacrificed. At first this idea met with furious objections, but hunger overruled. I left the final decision to the boys, so the books without covers were first to the flames— even Spiderman. Superman and the turtles were next. Our hot-dog sticks were flimsy and caught fire easily, so a few dogs were lost, but success was delicious. The buns had been left behind in the mad shuffle to get on the road, but several strategically placed Pringles held the hot dogs and served as an acceptable substitute. The comic-book blaze was hot and fast, but it seemed to burn the wieners very quickly. On closer inspection, I realized it was the ink from the printing that had turned them black, but by that time it was too late—we had eaten the lot. No one suffered any ill effects from those ink-fortified hot dogs, but I felt it best to keep that bit of information to myself...until now. Sorry, kids.

A multitude of burning comics dried the wood enough to give us a fantastic, albeit smoky, evening fire sufficient for a few ghost stories. It was getting dark, and after several feeble attempts, I realized I had no idea how to light the lantern. What was the purpose of that fragile little bag of fabric inside the glass? It immediately caught fire, burned to a crisp, and fell to bits. By that time, I was tired, and my matches were gone, but I remembered Hub had put a flashlight in my car last year. When the batteries began to fade, so did the giggling. It was time to go to sleep. The next morning, we woke early and went home hungry and grubby but happy.

We didn't give up! We went there to camp—and we stayed overnight!

Able to Leap Tall Buildings!

Reveling in the success of our recent camping trip, I felt my status rise from Fading Woman to Wonder Woman. I decided the best thing I could dedicate my newfound powers to would be to a much-needed increase in income. A friend of mine once told me the only way to earn a man's rate of pay was to do a man's job. She worked in the office of an automotive company in her pretty little suits and high heels and studied as a parts technician at night. Through hard work and hitting the books, she moved on to the shop floor with three new things: new coveralls, new steel-toed boots, and a new income bracket. The financial industry I was in didn't have that type of opportunity, and promotions weren't always awarded for hard work and dedication. There was a reason why the following joke circulated at our office Christmas party every year:

A blonde, a brunette, and a redhead are interviewing for the same investment position with the CEO. He gives them each a thousand dollars to invest and instructs them to meet with him again in thirty days. The blonde puts her money in a safe and doesn't touch it. The redhead spends the cash on clothes, shoes, and jewelry to impress her clients when she starts the new position. The brunette takes the grand and doubles her money through an insider-trading tip. A month later they are all back in the CEO's office. So which woman got the job? The one with the biggest boobs!

I had tried my hand at management several years before, when I accepted a one-year interim position with my firm. A trusted colleague told me that in the male-dominated management world we worked in, a good manager either had to have a prick or act like one. He said kind management was the worst type, and he felt I was too "nice" for the job. Since transgender surgery was out of the question, I decided I would take the other option. I would be a prick.

For twelve months, three days, and forty-five minutes, I had listened to, sympathized with, and tried to solve a mountain of staff problems and complaints, regarding all aspects of office politics. I had handled the numerous requests for time off—for everything from pet bereavement to an excruciating pimple on the ass or yeast infection—with as much fairness as common sense would allow. But I wasn't a good manager—I couldn't be a prick.

Since I knew management wasn't for me, the only other way to make more money was to increase my skills. That meant expanding my knowledge. Remember, girls, knowledge is a power tool. You can survive anything if you fill your toolbox with the right ones. Research, study, and learn what you need to know on how to advance within your field, or look at other career options. The courses I took gave me a better position and more money and eventually led to a great opportunity with the government. I didn't get the big bucks, but my new job had much better work flexibility and benefits.

When I enrolled in evening classes at the community college, I asked Hub to look after the kids two evenings a week. The body language was easy to read: his head nodded, the corners of his mouth turned up in a fake smile, but his eyes slid to the floor. After the second week of my classes, Hub started phoning with excuses about why he couldn't take care of the kids—working late, working late, and working late. Then he just stopped calling. I received a warning letter from the day care advising me that if Peewee was picked up late again, he would be kicked out. I knew I couldn't depend on Hub, and I couldn't force him to be responsible. I'd have to find another way.

I filled the fridge with casseroles and hired a teenager from the neighborhood to come in to feed and water the kids. She was expected to get them in bed before I got home from class to give me a few extra hours of study time.

My arrival home from class generally resulted in the standard charges against the babysitter:

"Mom, she hogged the phone all evening!"

"Mom, she played loud music, and I couldn't sleep!"

"Mom, she had friends in the house after we went to bed!"

"Mom, she was in your room with her boyfriend for a long time with the door locked!"

Children of the Corn

After babysitter number three was hired, my daughter complained that she was the one who made sure her brothers were washed, brushed, and in their PJs before climbing into bed while the sitter sat and watched TV or slept. When I got home one evening, I followed a trail of corn kernels up the stairs to the boys' closet, where I found a large bowl full of a disgusting, slimy mixture.

"It's a potion." Peewee beamed with pride.

"What did the babysitter say when she saw you doing this?"

"She told me to add the corn."

That was it; I was tired of paying someone for not supervising my children! My daughter met the age requirement for a babysitting course, so I enrolled her in "Sitting Safely." On registration night, I mentioned the course curriculum should also include instruction to the girls on sitting safely beside teenage boys—legs firmly crossed. My attempt at levity was met with blank stares. There is no sense of humor in babysitting class.

After three weeks, my daughter was presented with an elaborate, gold-embossed babysitting certificate, and I announced we would all celebrate at McDonalds. She argued that the boys didn't deserve to be included in her graduation dinner, since she would be the one doing all the work looking after them. I explained we all had to pull together for me to make a better life for us, and the boys would be working on their best behavior. Of course we didn't always have that Norman Rockwell kind of family unit, but I felt confident leaving my daughter in charge while I attended my college classes or took short excursions away from home.

The charges against the babysitter then changed to the following:

Plaintiff: "Mom, she ate my cookie!"
Defendant: "Well, I had to—there was only one left!"
Plaintiff: "Mom, she hid the remote!"
Defendant: "Well, I had to—he wanted to watch something stupid!"
Plaintiff: "Mom, she turned the light out and left me in the dark!"
Defendant: "Well, I had to—he hid in the toy box, and I couldn't find him!"

Mystery Meat

I thought the new babysitting arrangement was going quite well (except for the fudge-on-the-ceiling incident), so I accepted an invitation to the home of a coworker one evening for the proud showing of her firstborn child. After supper, I left the popcorn on the counter, grabbed my coat, and headed for the door without looking back.

It was wonderful to see the happy, young mother with her bundle of joy, reveling in the new sense of self-importance the baby had given her. When I looked at the beaming new father, I couldn't help but wonder if he too would leave when that smile wore off. My experience told me that would probably happen after the second or third child was born. I stared at his toothy grin and imagined what the future held for this couple. New Daddy won't be as excited at the arrival of yet another mouth to feed. He'll read the paper in the delivery room and won't enjoy the smell of barf on his shirts the way he did with baby number one. When his wife has a nursing-bra malfunction at a staff party, he'll stay and let her go home by herself. After the last baby is weaned, he'll complain that her boobs don't look as perky as when they were first married. He'll start working late and staying out with the boys more often. Then he'll run off with his secretary.

I glared at New Daddy as he handed me a cup of coffee and set down a tray of snacks with a flourish. Testosterone filled the room when he announced that he'd made the sausage all by himself from a deer he had murdered the week before. I politely informed him that I was not a fan of wild game and braced myself for his inevitable response.

"But deer sausage is good. You just need to try it—you'll like it!" he insisted.

"I have, and I don't," I said.

"But this one is different. It's better than any you've tried before. I like mine without any added beef or pork."

"I like mine without any deer."

I had met these types of overzealous casing-stuffers before. They give the term "sausage fest" a whole new meaning. All of them belong to a fraternity dedicated to converting you into a wild-sausage lover. And this guy would not give up. Finally, I picked up a piece of the vile-looking stuff along with a cracker and some cheese. New Daddy stared at me with an expectant grin as I skillfully palmed the sausage into my napkin and munched the cracker with exaggerated enthusiasm. I knew what was coming next.

"Well?" New Daddy grinned.

I chewed slowly and motioned to him that my mouth was full. He waited.

"How did you like it?" he blurted.

After a long, thoughtful, chewing pause, I said, "I must say, if I was a person who liked deer sausage, I might like it."

New Daddy looked stunned and quickly excused himself to let the dog in while New Mommy glared at me as though I'd hit her husband over the head with a big fat chunk of mystery meat. Just then, a cute bundle of fluff bounded into the room, through our awkward moment, and crashed onto my lap. The little dog forced his nose into my hand holding the balled-up, meaty napkin.

"Foofer, get over here—leave her alone!" yelled New Daddy.

I reached to pat his furry little head, and he lunged at my sausage-scented fingers.

"Foofer, bad dog—get into your kennel!"

My conscience still bears the imprint of that sad, fuzzy face and the memory of poor Foofer, relegated to his cage for the rest of the evening.

I arrived home after the boys were in bed and whispered to my daughter, "How was babysitting tonight?"

Before she could answer, Peewee came tearing out of his room and clamped onto my leg. "She put me up on the fridge and wouldn't take me down!"

"Well, I had to—he was bugging me!"

I hoisted Peewee up over my shoulder and headed down the hall toward the Winnie the Pooh door. "So, I guess it went pretty well then."

3

HERE I GO AGAIN ON MY OWN

Hello Reader,
I was single in a couples' world. You might discover when your ex replaces you with someone else, friends take sides—and not always yours. There are many red flags to remind you you're not a couple anymore.

Red Flags:

- You can throw out your "Two can dine for $19.99" coupons.
- You are excluded from the neighborhood block party committee but asked to make the same monetary contribution as the year before.
- You avoid Sweetheart Night at the movies.
- You send flowers to yourself.

- You empty the kids' piggy banks and hire a drag queen to crash your ex-husband's office party and hit on him.
- You sit alone at family funerals.

A Members-Only Club

One of the hardest things I had to cope with after the breakdown of my marriage was the feeling that everyone in the world was one half of a couple except me. Overnight, I had lost my entire source of support: financial, parental, and social. It was like switching from the comfort of a tandem bike to the balancing act of a unicycle. My family considered divorce a four-letter word and social stigma. Even Canada Geese mate for life. Fair-weather married friends started to fade away. They wanted to do things with their "own kind." I began to suspect my husband had quickly joined that couples' alliance again while I was still on my own, singing along with Whitesnake. One early-morning phone call from a dear, sweet, married friend of mine put an end to any doubts about that.

Before that ringing phone invaded my Saturday morning, I had been trying my best to sleep in. It had been a long, busy week at the office, followed by frenzied evenings of Little League, Girl Guides, Hamburger Helper, and homework. I had looked forward to a Saturday sleep-in almost as much as that Hawaiian vacation Hub had promised me. Hawaii never came. There were always more pressing emergencies—a big-screen TV, new golf clubs, a better BBQ than the neighbor. An even bigger screen.

The weekly sleep-in was my sanctuary, my sanity saver. These days that ritual was even more important—less time to think. Think about Hub. Think about money. Think about my failures.

The bedroom was cool, the shades were down, and, most important, the door was closed. I had trained the kids, with military precision, to fix their own cereal and watch television cartoons with strict volume control. This routine was fortified by the Saturday Ten Rule, which was the equivalent of martial law. It meant absolutely no entry to my inner sanctum before 10:00 a.m., except under extreme emergency circumstances: pestilence, plague, or possible loss of limb.

I was drifting along in my hazy half sleep with thoughts of unfinished housework and hosting the dreaded afternoon playdate with a couple of neighborhood kids. At first, I thought I'd imagined the soft, tentative knock, so I dug deeper into my wonderful, warm cocoon. There was one brief, blessed moment of silence, and then came a loud banging, followed by, "*Mom*!"

I pushed out of bed and staggered to the door, looking like the wreck of the *Hesperus*.

"Remember the Saturday Ten Rule?" I croaked and squinted against the sunlight's rude intrusion through the hall window.

The answer came in the form of Middle Child's outstretched arms pushing a small cage under my nose.

"I think my hamster's gonna have babies," he said.

Trying to keep a grip on to my patience, my words came out with slow deliberation. "No, the guy at the pet store told us these hamsters are brothers."

I was not in the mood for the little talk about the birds and bees at that moment. But, on closer examination, I could see Little Ham's abdomen had a suspicious bulge, and Big Ham was cowering in the corner of the cage with a guilty look on his furry face.

"Honey, put the cage back in your room, and we'll take him to the Pet Shop Boys where we bought him, after Mommy's sleep-in."

"We're gonna take him back?"

"No, we're not going to return him—or her—we'll just let them have a look and make sure there's nothing wrong with that big tummy—after Mommy's sleep-in."

I flopped back into the bed and burrowed down under my big, blue blanket of sadness. A few minutes later, the sound of rapid, persistent knocking drove my head under the pillow, and I let out a loud groan.

"They're here!" the three kids shouted in unison, through the door.

"Who's here?" I asked. "I said no friends in the house until this afternoon!"

"Not friends," my daughter shrieked, "the baby hamsters!"

I crept from my down-filled refuge and opened the door to the sight of the ugliest little pink creatures, cradled gently in Middle Child's hands.

The last thing I needed was something else to take care of. I started to think it was time for Little, Big, and ugly Baby Hams to sleep with the fishes in the big toilet bowl in the sky. I pushed past kids and rodents to the bathroom and closed the door. Most days I did my best thinking there, but this was not going to be one of those days. My thought of sending the Ham family to a watery grave was interrupted by the shrill ring of the telephone.

"Don't answer the—"

"Hello, who is this?" I heard Peewee's sweet little voice.

"Put down that phone!" I screamed as I pulled up my new Fruit of the Looms.

"No, he doesn't live here anymore. No, she's having a poop."

I rushed out and grabbed the receiver to find one of my long-lost married friends on the line. Mrs. Married Friend immediately launched into a nonstop news flash of what Hub had been doing lately. The phone couldn't disguise her delight when she realized she was the first to tell me that my husband was seeing someone else. *Yeah, seeing her brains out!* I learned that the other woman was called Dee-Dee, and judging by my husband's preoccupation with mammary glands, it was easy to surmise the source of that nick-name. I'm sure Hub thought he had won the big prize. *Yeah, the booby prize!* Mrs. Married Friend gushed on with all the gory details of how D-Cup had gone out of town with Hub on a business trip the previous month. *Yeah, monkey business!*

"Oh, you're so wonderfully kind to take the time to call me, but you didn't have to bother," I said sweetly. "I was there with them—we're swingers. Hub's really into that kind of thing, but of course I'm out of it now, because it's just for couples—like you and Charlie. Wait, don't hang up. Let me give you more information."

The most painful part was the realization that Hub had some-one waiting in the wings all along.

I wanted to contact Acme for an anvil to drop on Hub's junk or enroll in a firearms course. Instead, I started watching reruns of *The Sopranos,* and my recurring dream began to include James Gandolfini. Unfortunately, in my dreams, he was never a gangster or hit man ready to exact revenge on my husband. He was my pa-perboy or the pizza delivery guy.

The Rise and Fall of D-Cup!

During the first year of the marriage breakdown, our lives were marked with even more sadness when both of Hub's parents passed away. My mother-in-law was first to go, and her death was sudden and unexpected, on the eve of her retirement. Patricia had never been the doting grandmother type, but she had been a big part of my life since I'd lost my own mother when I was a teenager. She had been furious with Hub when he left me, and her passing meant not only did I lose a mother figure but one of my few al-lies in the divorce battle. The news of her death was a shock, but during the past year, I had become so practiced at holding myself together that I had no tears to shed for Patricia.

A cloying smell of roses hung in the air of the funeral chapel as I took a seat near the back on that sad, snowy day. The grieving family was seated together at the front near a small ornate box with a large picture of a smiling Patricia next to it. I could see D-Cup's giant, blond head resting on the shoulder of Hub's blazer—the one I'd given him for his birthday. My gaze wandered from Hub's Harris Tweed shoulder to the back of his head, and I noticed it looked different somehow. That thinning patch of hair seemed a bit fuller. *Oh my god, is that a perm?*

Once again, I found myself pushing down a church-giggle rising up from my gut like bad gas. But this time, the laughter stuck in my throat in a big lump of sadness.

My father-in-law was in a state of stoic numbness as I offered my condolences after the service. With great apprehension, I accepted his offer to go back to the house for coffee with the family. When I arrived, a few of Hub's old high school football friends were attacking the buffet table like a flock of picnic seagulls. Those guys had been close to Patricia when they all hung around the house in their glory days. None of them spoke to me. I hadn't fit into their crowd back then, and I sure as hell didn't now.

I couldn't help but notice D-Cup sitting alone, while most of my ex-husband's attention centered on one particular former football star—the head cheerleader. As I sipped the strong, black coffee, I pondered what duties would be expected of a position with the title "head." When Hub's sister handed me a rose from the casket flowers, I felt D-Cup's eyes shooting daggers at me from across the room. That felt bad.

It was time for me to leave. While searching for my shoes through the pile of footwear at the door, I recognized the Western boots Hub was currently favoring during his newly acquired urban-cowboy phase. As I bent down to pull on my pumps, I broke the stem off my casket rose and shoved the thorny twig down into the toe of that tacky snakeskin boot. That felt good.

Six weeks later, I found myself mourning my father-in-law. I felt the loss but still had no tears. Once again, my ex-husband sat in the front pew in his tweed blazer, with a woman's head resting on his shoulder. This time it was a brunette head...Miss Head Cheerleader's head. D-Cup had been tossed onto the scrap heap beside me. Others would follow.

A Mere Flesh Wound!

The next day was Middle Child's birthday, so I picked up an angel-food cake mix on my way home from the funeral. Birthday boy had invited half a dozen of his classmates to our house after school, and right then I couldn't think of anything worse than a bunch of screaming kids tearing around the house. Hub hadn't offered any kind of help with the celebration, so party fare would have to be basic this year—hot dogs, cake, and ice cream. I spent the entire evening putting up decorations and preparing games, snacks, and goody bags. By eleven o'clock, Betty Crocker's instructions had finally taken me to the last step in the cake-baking process: "Remove from oven, and immediately turn pan upside down onto glass bottle." The only glass bottle I could find was the last beer at the back of the fridge. My obligation to drink it was for a good cause, and I was half-asleep when my head hit the pillow. As I drifted into dreamland, I heard a faint, familiar sound. I recognized it from time spent at my daughter's home-economics class. It was the sound of an undercooked angel food cake spilling its guts out onto the kitchen counter.

The floodgates finally opened: tears for the loss of the cake, for the loss of my in-laws, and for the loss of my marriage. The protective shell I had carefully layered over the fragile core of my emotions was destroyed by undercooked pastry.

I had no time to bake another cake and no money to buy one. I didn't even have time to change my clothes from work the next day before the little party guests began to arrive. I put all the food on the table and told them to help themselves—hot dogs, condiments, a bucket of ice cream, and an assortment of desert toppings. Then I kicked off my heels and flopped into the nearest chair with a cup of coffee, while the birthday boy and his friends started a contest to see who could make the weirdest ice cream sundae. Chocolate fudge with relish, pineapple, and ketchup—and the winner, marshmallow mustard! Ben and Jerry would have cringed. I was just about to present the prize for the most disgusting dessert when the front door opened. In walked Hub, pushing a new bike with one hand and holding a beautifully decorated cake in the other.

What a bastard!

The whole party was busy admiring the new bike when Hub turned to leave and quietly informed me he wouldn't be able to take the kids to a theme park in the city that weekend, as promised. I knew he expected me to break the news to them, so I blocked his escape route and called the kids over to tell them their father had something to say. Hub squirmed like a worm, but I stood my ground and stared at him like a gunfighter at high noon. He was trapped, with no way out. I had the warped idea that I could appeal to his yellow streak, and he'd be too much of a chicken shit to back out of their weekend plans. Instead, he used the opportunity to announce that he was moving in with Miss Head Cheerleader.

Three confused little faces turned toward me. There were no words. I just stood there watching myself in slow motion as I shoved a wooden stake through Hub's heart and ran down the street screaming all the profanity I had pent up since the day he walked out. When I stopped running, I looked down and saw the stake had pierced my own chest.

Rub-a-Dub-Dub, Three Kids in a Tub

I wasn't sure what type of social etiquette dictated a celebration of Hub's new cohabitation and assumed that Hallmark didn't use the type of wording I was looking for. So I decided on a dead-plant bouquet for the happy couple.

Frustration with my situation at home was piling up, and I made the mistake of unloading a bit of it at work. My coworkers were eager to help—not with the kids or a home-cooked meal but with advice. Lots and lots of advice. I was informed that "I should play the cards I was dealt."

"That sounds like a great idea, Ruth," I replied, "but the cards I'm playing with are all bills and past-due notices, and the deck is stacked against me because my ex-husband is the joker!"

I didn't expect sympathy; the only place I ever found that was in the dictionary between "sex" and "syphilis." I was swimming in a cesspool of emotion, but I knew becoming a victim of self-pity was a luxury I couldn't afford. I had to put on my big-girl panties and get on with it.

My new resolve had just started to raise my head above the emotional waters when the washer broke down. For the next few evenings, I had the kids scrub their gym uniforms in the tub, and I threw my undies in the bath with Peewee. That laundry technique came to an abrupt end when he freaked out as the pantyhose ballooned to gigantic proportions under water pressure from the tap. Freudian counselors would rub their hands together over that.

On Saturday afternoon, the kids dragged our laundry baskets into Scrub-a-Dub, and I plugged a handful of coins into the gaping maw of the greedy machines. The bulletin board was jammed with notices and looked like a good place to find a used washer. I scanned the bits of paper and saw the usual: TRANS-CAMARO FOR SALE and a GET OUT OF HELL FREE card courtesy of a Bible-thumping religious freak. I forgot all about looking for a washer when my eyes stopped on a bright-yellow poster. It advertised a family-style music festival at a ranch outside of town on Sunday. And it was free. I didn't notice the weight of the wet laundry as I lifted the baskets into the back of my car and headed home to the dryer. I was thinking of a much-needed afternoon of music and relaxation. In my mind, we were already on the road and on our way to having some fun!

The Big-Bag Theory

Sunday morning was full of promise. I packed a cooler with the usual kid-friendly provisions and shoehorned it into my little hatchback, along with lawn chairs, blankets, bats, and balls. Hub used to tell me the little white car looked like an egg, but that day it was a stuffed omelet. The ranch was tucked into the rolling foothills, and as I steered Eggy through the scenic countryside, I promised myself we would come out this way more often. We were on our way to having some fun!

But bright sunshine and no air-conditioning soon resulted in some hot and cranky children. I needed ninety SPF sunscreen for the back of their necks or some type of sunshade. I've always been a firm believer that a large, well-stocked purse can take care of anything. That day I couldn't find anything in my handbag to shield the kids from the relentless sun, although it gave me the opportunity to get rid of a half-eaten apple, some cheese slices, and a squashed, dubious-looking brown sandwich. We stopped at a service station for some cold drinks, and I bought a roll of stretchy black electrical tape, which I used to fasten a road map to the inside of the back window to block the sun. I didn't understand why the wrapper claimed it was electric because it clearly didn't have any wires, but it worked just fine to keep the map in place. Soon we were back on the road and on our way to having fun.

"He took my Transformer!"

"Give the toy back to him!"

"Wah…he threw it in my face!"

"Apologize to your brother. Now give him yours!"

"Why? I didn't throw it that hard!"

"I have to pee."

"Are we there yet?"

"I have to pee *bad*!"

"Will you all please shut up?"

Sorry, ladies, but I believe if you have stretch marks, you're entitled to say that to your kids once in their lifetimes. I had just noticed one of the gauges on the dashboard of my car was pointing to a bright-red line. I couldn't remember if it had always been like that, and, for one crazy moment, I thought the tape I'd used to fasten the map to the back window had something to do with it. Then I saw steam pouring out from under the hood. I pulled over and made the kids go stand in a grain field while I flagged down a passing car. The Good Samaritan flipped open the hood and poked around.

He looked at the large handbag on my shoulder and laughed. "Got any electrician's tape in that thing?"

It was my turn to laugh as I produced the sticky black roll from the bottom of my purse. Good Sam wrapped the tape around something, and we were finally back on the road, on our way to fun.

A Fine Feathered Friend

We were late getting to the ranch, and a group of people had already gathered on a hillside, which formed perfect bleachers for the occasion. Amps and speakers were set up on a flatbed truck, and a couple of bearded longhairs were tuning up on the makeshift stage. The Hairs did a great job of warming up the crowd. Next up was a bluegrass band, fronted by a hairy-armpitted flower-child nymph jiggling her tambourine and tits. I settled our blanket and cooler at a spot high up on the hill and warned Middle Child not to wander too far. He was responsible for his age but was not a savvy country boy. Music had recently become my source of respite, and as it drifted over me, I could feel the pressured grip of the past several weeks start to loosen. I leaned back to soak up the warm sun and noticed a million tiny wildflowers all around me. Taking a deep breath, I inhaled the smell of fresh grass—both nature's and homegrown.

I was struck by the caliber of talented musicians and looked forward to the day with an evening bonfire finale. A woman around my age was snapping pictures with a professional-looking camera, so I asked her to take some shots of me and the kids. It was time to start a new photo album.

A man with a huge Stetson and a belly to match stepped up to the mic and asked for children to come to the stage. Middle Child ran up to the blanket with a couple of other kids to get a drink and announced they were entering a chicken-chasing contest. I watched the little ones gather around Stetson Man as he released a small, scraggly feathered creature to the wild. It ran off with surprising speed, and the kids took off after it at top speed, screaming and zigzagging over the hillside. Stretched out on the blanket, I could see the chicken chasers move in and out of view in hot pursuit of their prey. I didn't think any of them had much of a chance of catching the poor little thing and was silently cheering for the chicken.

A glam metal band took the stage and picked up the volume and pace, and a guy with a long ZZ Top beard sitting on a motorcycle leaned over to offer me a puff. At that moment, Middle Child raced up and plunked a wire cage down on the blanket. It was filled with furious flapping, and Peewee began to scream.

I peered into the cage and saw two beady little eyes staring back at me through the bars of the wire prison. A moment later, I felt my mouth completely unhinge as I noticed a mass of deep, ugly scratches covering Middle Child's legs. The bloody lacerations seemed insignificant to him, and his staccato words tumbled out at warp speed.

"I won...the contest...and...the prize...is a rooster!" Then he caught his breath and announced that he'd named him Rupert.

A small congratulatory crowd of kids gathered around as Stetson Man pinned a red ribbon on Middle Child's puffed-out little chest, handed him a small bag of feed, and walked away. I stood speechless among the bedlam as my peaceful afternoon imploded.

The drive home was silent. Peewee was asleep in his car seat, and my daughter had stayed at the bonfire with friends. There were no words left in my arsenal against keeping Rupert. I could see Middle Child in the rearview mirror, with one protective hand on the cage beside him and the other examining the bandages on his shins, like badges of honor. Long spurs on the rooster's feet told me Rupert was a bantam, and, when cornered, he had used those spikes on my son's skinny legs. Middle Child argued to keep Rupert in his room, but we finally came to a compromise. The rooster would live in the garage—temporarily. It would be Middle Child's job to make sure Rupert had food and water and to supervise him in the backyard every day after school until a proper home could be found for him. Secretly, I hoped the foul little fellow would run or fly away to someone's dinner table. Judging by the size of him, that person would have to be on a diet.

The following week, I was jolted from my dream each morning at sunrise to the sound of Rupert crowing in the garage. He would also crow after dark if the light next to the garage window was turned on, and it became a great source of amusement for all three kids. I was missing sleep and getting nervous about Mrs. Busybody next door. She had threatened to call animal control, so a scramble to find Rupert a permanent home began in earnest. A call to the farm where we bought free-range eggs gave us the perfect solution. They had a small market for fertilized eggs, so Rupert would be a working rooster. At first Middle Child had mixed feelings about seeing his fine feathered friend leave him. He had gained increased status in his class by being the only kid to have a pet rooster and was conducting afterschool tours of the garage. But he'd also grown tired of supervising Rupert's backyard privileges and the yucky cleanup. He agreed that the country home was a good idea.

The following Saturday morning, we all arrived at the farm and were welcomed by a friendly bark from Ozzie, the resident canine greeter. Rupert's cage was placed inside a fence that held a small coop and a group of fat fluffy hens with feathered feet. We all watched anxiously as the cage door opened and Rupert strutted out. He looked so small. After a quick survey of his new surroundings, he scratched a bit, let out a lusty crow, and dropped a large turd. It was plain to see he would be cock of the walk.

Several weeks later, we decided to drive out to the farm for some eggs and to check on Rupert. When we got there, we were stopped by a handwritten sign on the locked gate: "Egg Farm Closed." I could see several men in odd-looking masks and papery white suits spraying the coops. They weren't painting, and I had a bad feeling when I noticed there wasn't a single chicken in sight. We raced home to call the farm and were told the place was infested with something called red mite. All the chickens had been lost within three days. Middle Child was jumping up and down, pulling at my arm as I asked the farmer about Rupert. We were surprised to learn that he was the lone survivor and was living quite comfortably in the straw-filled doghouse. Ozzie had apparently given up his home without a fuss, but I couldn't help but wonder if those lethal talons of Rupert's might have had something to do with that. After a while, I got a flyer in the mail from the farm. They were selling eggs again, and Rupert's position was reinstated with a new harem of hens.

The cholesterol hype reduced egg consumption at our house, and Rupert was rarely thought of until years later, when the phone call came. We all piled into the old white-and-rust hatchback and drove out to the farm. Middle Child—or MC, as he preferred to be called—was behind the wheel with a shiny new learner's permit in his back pocket. Old Ozzie struggled to his feet and wagged in recognition of our somber faces. The farmer was waiting for us beside the chicken coop with a shoebox in his hands. I put my hand on MC's shoulder as he stepped forward to take the box. Then he walked over to a freshly dug hole in the ground.

4

A CHANGE WILL DO YOU GOOD

My Dear Reader,
Did you ask yourself why he left? Did you start to
question what was wrong with you? I started to see
red flags that told me it was time for a change.

Red Flags:

- Your "couture" isn't so "haute" anymore.
- Most of your cosmetics expired two years ago.
- The only eye shadow you own is electric blue.
- Babysitters don't steal your clothes anymore or even try
  them on.
- The peach fuzz on your upper lip has turned into a Fu
  Manchu.
- Your handbag has a new strap made of duct tape.

- Last year's winter boots have been called into service as fashion footwear.

The Crying Game

Within several months of our separation, my ex-husband was already on his second relationship, and I hadn't even adjusted to being on my own. Would I ever meet someone? Would I want to? But an even bigger question plagued me. Who would want a thirty-something woman dragging a huge breakup ball and chain and three kids behind her? My self-confidence had taken a real shit kicking, and a jabbing little voice of insecurity was using my ego as a punching bag. A few more rounds of self-doubt and I'd be down for the count.

Each evening when I ran out of energy, I would try to wipe my mind clean of life's garbage for that day. Then, I'd sit down to watch someone else's garbage on TV—*Married with Children*. Al and Peg Bundy were the only people I knew who were even more fucked-up than Hub and me...but they were still together.

Since the botched angel-food cake incident, I couldn't listen to my favorite tunes anymore while doing housework without crying. The only CDs Hub had left behind were the ones we had listened to together. They were songs we sang while dancing around the living room after a few cocktails—Bryan Adams, Elton John, and Bon Jovi. When I heard them now, I would end up with the vacuum in one hand, a Kleenex in the other, and snot running down my face. During one of those blubbering episodes, I realized I had never had any music of my own. I hadn't bought anything for just me—always something Hub would like. A quick trip to Song Swap got rid of the old musical memories and started some new ones. "Girls Just Wanna Have Fun," "Dancing Queen," "Girls' Night Out," and I couldn't forget "Highway to Hell."

But the mascara kept running. Each morning my pillow was crusted with dried tears and felt like it was stuffed with prickly penguin feathers. I made a puddle on the floor of my car if a bug splattered against my windshield or I heard Human League on the radio asking, "Don't You Want Me, Baby?" The sad little IKEA lamp turned me into mush when I saw it being kicked to the curb on TV. I knew how that felt. And the crying was ugly—no lady-like sniffling for me. I sounded like a colicky baby and looked like a crumpled shrunken-head centerfold from *National Geographic*. So my tears fell in private. I knew I had to pull myself together when the kids started shoving pieces of paper under the bathroom door scrawled with, "Are we having supper today?" and "What time should we go to bed?"

Dummies for Stress Management

I would paste a mask of comedy on at work, but the face of tragedy always lurked behind. I chewed my nails until my fingers looked terminal, and there were no more staff lunches in trendy cafes for me until I'd finished paying my lawyer's retainer. I was terrible company anyway, so I stayed at the office, drank coffee, and nibbled at the peanut-butter-and-jelly sandwich I brought from home. That daily routine picked the scab from a festering memory that had never quite healed.

When my daughter was fifteen months old, my first husband had passed away suddenly with no life insurance for me and the baby. As a single man, he had purchased insurance with his mother as beneficiary, and we didn't think to change it when we got married. The company's agent came to our little apartment one evening with documentation to put my name on the policy. But that night we were busy packing up a feverish baby to take to the emergency medical clinic. We promised to contact the insurance agent when our daughter had recovered from her ear infection. We didn't.

I have a clear recollection of the journey to the clinic that night with our whimpering little bundle. Wayne had turned to me and said, "You know, if anything happened to me, my mom would give you the insurance money." She didn't.

That error in judgment resulted in some lean years for my daughter and me, with a lot of peanut-butter-and-jelly sandwiches for both of us. And there I was...eating PB and J. Again.

My mounting stress reached breaking point at work one morning after I had dealt with a notoriously difficult client. Without a word, I left my desk and took the stairs down to the document vault in the basement. In the middle of that gray, musty-smelling room, I stood in a corner and screamed as loud as I could. I managed a few minutes of temporary solitude in the lunchroom to pull myself together before a well-meaning coworker came in. Lily handed me a cup of coffee along with a self-help book on stress management. She said it was guaranteed to make anyone feel better. I knew she meant well, but when I told her I didn't even have time to read the newspaper, she gave me a recording of the book so I could listen to it in my car. I took the tape and assured her I'd listen to it and try to keep an open mind. Then she held out her hand and asked me for five bucks.

Lily had emphasized the tape was guaranteed to make me feel better, so I decided to try it out on my drive home from work that day. It would be a perfect test since I was in a nasty mood from dealing with the demanding client, as well as the exposed underwire in my worn-out bra that had been burrowing into my left boob all day. Lily's glowing testimonial for the tape had promised to change all that, so I should be feeling better before I picked Peewee up from day care. It was guaranteed.

At five o'clock I popped the tape into the player, pushed the button, and listened to the instructional prelude. It recommended finding a comfortable spot in complete solitude and taking a few deep breaths before beginning. My setting was perfect. I was alone in my car and had been sneaking a few cigarettes at the end of each day, so I lit up and inhaled several of the prescribed deep breaths before leaving the parking lot.

I drove for about five minutes, listening to the monotone voice of some self-righteous man droning on and on about how I should not allow myself a single moment of anger. Blah, blah, blah. When I'd heard enough, I hit eject, rolled down the window, and tossed the tape out. What a bunch of sanctimonious bullshit! I had a right to my anger, and I'd let go of it when I was damned good and ready. But it wasn't going to be that day. Anger was the only driving force I had to keep me from buckling under the crush of work, finances, kids, school, house, yard, dog, shopping, birthdays—and being on my own.

But I had to admit, the so-called self-help tape definitely delivered its guarantee. Seeing those bits of broken plastic in my rearview mirror, glistening in the sun as they bounced off the pavement, made me feel a lot better.

The following week, I welcomed another stress-relieving diversion from the work treadmill. We had experienced a large increase in customer traffic when our firm began a contest for a free trip to Cuba. Employees weren't eligible to participate, but we were all tasked with promoting the offer, which included a huge advertising campaign, complete with tacky posters and tourist wear. Our biggest challenge in the promotion was a huge, white inflatable airplane suspended above our customer service desk. It had a slow leak and looked like a terminally ill seagull by the end of the day. Since it was an integral part of the contest advertising, each staff member took turns blowing it back up each morning before the doors were opened to the public.

By the last day of the contest, our plane had been losing more air every day, and Lily volunteered to leave her post at reception to service the plane. She kicked off her heels, hitched up the ties on her flowery fuchsia wraparound skirt, and jumped up on the counter to give the deflating 747 its daily blow job. As I watched Lily up on her perch, I noticed a long line of disgruntled customers pacing outside, so I unlocked the door and opened it a crack to tell them we would be ready for business in a few minutes. I immediately lost control of the crowd as they pushed through the door and charged into the room.

A startled Lily stepped back onto the hem of her skirt, which snapped the flimsy ties and launched her off the counter with the plane firmly clenched between her teeth. The room was paralyzed as all eyes watched our dedicated concierge maneuver a successful liftoff and safe landing for herself and the aircraft. The same could not be said for the skirt. It crash-landed onto the floor at Lily's feet in a heap of flowery, fuchsia wreckage.

Life of Pie

I had always maintained a long-standing on-again, off-again sordid love affair with food, so the next phase of the emotional carnival ride of my marriage breakdown came as no surprise to me. The food roller coaster.

When Hub left, I initially survived on black coffee and a few backyard cigarettes. After that, my grocery bags were bulging with Twinkies, Ding Dongs, Pringles, and all manner of chocolate. I told myself quantity buying was economical, since my selections likely had enough preservatives to last at least ten years. It soon became apparent that shelf life would not be an issue, so in a gallant effort toward stock control, I enlisted my two older children to hide the goodies from me. It was obvious that idea wasn't going to work when I began ransacking the house after they were asleep. Then my search sank to an all-time low—under the beds. My only score there was an abundance of dust rabbits (too big to be called bunnies), some mismatched gum-encrusted socks, and several unfinished homework assignments with a corresponding number of notes from teachers regarding unfinished homework assignments. I tore the cupboards and closets apart until I hit pay dirt. Noisy cellophane packages had to be opened with great care so as not to wake the kids and expose my dirty little secret. Or have to share with them. I needed to pay special attention when drinking soda, since Peewee could hear the sound of a pop can opening at one hundred paces. When the feeding frenzy was over, I'd sit in the huge pile of discarded wrappers and cry.

Nothing was safe. I even stole my son's Halloween candy and let his sister take the blame. When I admitted this transgression to Barb at work, she pulled me aside and dropped a confession bomb of her own. She had been on the way to a family funeral, with her stomach in knots, and decided a quick detour through a fast-food drive-in for a loaded burger would make her feel better. Barb described in great detail how the guilty aroma of her indulgence seemed to hang in air throughout the service. Later, while giving her condolences to the family, she noticed a large, delicious-looking slice of pickle stuck to the lapel of her suit. I asked her how she survived such embarrassment, and she told me she shrugged it off by convincing herself she could pass it off as some kind of avant-garde scratch-and-sniff jewelry. I needed that type of attitude. I wanted to walk up to Bubba, Bat-Woman, and Mary Hard-Faced-Bitch with pickles all over the front of my shirt and tell them to fuck off!

It Ain't Easy Bein' Me

Self-confidence isn't easy to regain when you've let someone take it from you. The bathroom mirror became my enemy. One small conciliation was that my laugh lines weren't getting any deeper. They weren't being used. A critical little inner voice inventoried my flaws and forced me to confront the body my husband had discarded: thunder thighs, turkey neck, Bob Hope nose. *Okay, enough—shut up, already!* I would turn on the shower and only look in the mirror after steam filled the room and blurred my face. When the fog lifted, I'd squint at the reflection and press my palms to my cheeks to pull back the skin on my face. Then I'd run a finger along the ugly surgical scar on my throat. The thing I remember most about that thyroid operation was eating nothing but green Jell-O for three days during my hospital stay. For some reason they didn't serve any flavor other than lime, and it tasted like Mr. Clean. I still hate green Jell-O.

When the incision on my throat finally healed, it was an angry-looking red and matched my attitude toward the surgeon. Insensitive people would sometimes ask me about the scar. That made me uncomfortable, so I had devised a safeguard for my feelings. I'd tell them when I was born, my mother thought I was so ugly that she switched heads with the baby in the next cot. I needed such a safeguard for my bruised and battered self-image now.

I needed a change. It was time to call the girls!

Off with the Old

These girls were a couple of women my age who became part of my life because they were kindred spirits in a similar situation. They replaced most of my old friends who had run for the protective cover of their marriages when they heard Hub and I had split up. The three of us made a bit of a motley crew, but, for the first time since the divorce hit the fan, I had two people in my life whom I could truly depend on. They were friends you could trust to tell you when you had a big gob of mascara on your face or the back of your skirt was tucked into your pantyhose. Up to that point, I thought only Smith & Wesson would be my BFFs.

I'd met Danni in line at the Java Shop when a handful of coins slipped from my shaky fingers and bounced all over the slippery black tiles. A lot of things in my life were shaky around that time. She looked stunning in bright-yellow yoga togs, and I giggled as she struck a quasi-downward dog right there in the middle of the coffee shop to help pick up my change. With her height, that position made her look like a giraffe splaying its legs to drink from a pond. She followed me to my table with her coffee, and, by the end of our second cup, I had a good friend.

The more I came to know her, the more I found Danni was everything I was not. Her thoughts and emotions were up front, not tucked behind a mask, where I kept mine. I could never expose my vulnerabilities for fear of being completely destroyed, and I'd nurtured a tough exterior to keep a lot of my true feelings secured. Danni's openness was the key to unlock those reservations. She was bubbly enough to have champagne running through her veins. But that carefree, upbeat exterior housed a firm don't-mess-with-me core, and the tone of her voice could give a deserving recipient the middle finger without her moving a muscle. She had testicular fortitude, didn't take any crap from anyone, and always seemed to get what she wanted—like a man, but in a gorgeous woman's body. I learned she'd come out of her divorce a lot better off than I was going to. She'd managed to keep her house and enough cash for a boob job. Her ex-husband paid child support plus alimony—regularly. She often talked about getting a job for extra money, but there always seemed to be something keeping her from working—usually some kind of "class." That term was interchangeable with any number of things she was doing...working out at the gym, seeing a counselor, or volunteering at her son's school.

All men wanted Danni. She usually ignored them, and, of course, that made them want her more. If she was interested, her words were wrapped in satin sheets when she spoke. These men always considered themselves her irresistible seducers, but, in reality, they were the seduced. A few months after we met, she was treating me to lunch at her favorite bistro near my office where a group of white collars were having a three-martini lunch. They were desperate to get Danni's attention, but she continued to push the food around on her plate like she always did and refused to offer them even the slightest glance. In desperation, one of them got down on his hands and knees, in a beautiful Armani suit, crawled over to our table, and bit her on her leg. They dated for a few weeks.

I was fortunate to have a second wonderful friend enter my life as well. Jennifer became a voice of reason for me when I needed it most. We met at the outdoor music festival the day Rupert the rooster joined our household. She had a great way with a camera, and I had asked her to take some pictures of my newly downsized family unit. A week after the festival, I was wrangling the kids to the dinner table when Jennifer stopped by to drop off the photos. I invited her to pull up a plate of pasta, and she stayed to lend a hand with the cleanup. After the kids were in bed, we had coffee and talked into the night. I learned she was divorced with no children. I assumed she planned to keep it that way when I noticed the letters of the vanity plate on her 1972 Dodge Demon spelled IUD.

Jennifer was a little tangled mass of red hair, around five feet tall, but her shoes all had four-inch heels, which enabled her to exude a much larger presence. Quiet but not shy, she kept things close to her chest. Her business was freelance photography, supplemented by touch-up photo work for some lecherous old guy at a downtown studio at slave wages. Jennifer's work was extremely good, and her creative flair also showed in the Bohemian-style clothing and jewelry she wore, as well as her artsy studio apartment. The plain little bachelor flat had been transformed into a fabulous home, decorated with Jennifer's artwork, photographs, and numerous tropical plants. It was sparsely furnished, and we often sat on the floor since her two cats, Ike and Tina, owned the small couch. There was no television, and I learned to appreciate B. B. King, Robert Cray, and cold Chablis in that little haven. I loved being there.

When I decided it was time for a change, I called on Danni and Jennifer to help with my makeover. The girls were so enthused, they decided to go for new looks as well. Hub had promised to take the kids to a movie that evening, which left the three of us to carry out our beautification plans at my place. I knew Hub would fill the kids with movie junk food, and they should be fed before he picked them up, so I grabbed a loaf of bread and the industrial-size jar of Cheez Whiz from the fridge and started to make sandwiches.

Middle Child rushed in from the bathroom and held up his hands. "I ain't eating that!"

"You mean you are *not* eating that," I corrected. "And why not?"

"That's what I said. I know what cheese is, and I know what whiz is…and it ain't that."

Hair to Dye For

The girls and I put our heads together and decided to start from the top. Since we were all on tight budgets, we agreed if we shared one blond hair dye, the three of us could get beautiful highlights from the price of one box. There is only one bit of advice I can give to women who think they can create a great new look on the cheap. Do *not* shop for hair products at a pharmacy next to a liquor store. Coconut rum and a tight budget are not a good combination in the pursuit of beauty.

We poured some drinks as soon as we got back home with our purchases and set the box of Bodacious Blond on the table. The three of us sat down and stared at it like the Holy Grail. Jennifer finally grabbed the box, ripped it open, and snapped on the flimsy plastic gloves.

Danni poured more drinks, and we each donned one of the prized T-shirts Hub had left behind in his hasty escape from our marriage. The three of us crowded into the bathroom, where Jennifer revealed her amazing skill with hair. She even gave us a quick trim before applying what we soon learned was weapons-grade peroxide.

I poured a few more drinks and set the timer on the stove to let Bodacious Blond work her magic. When I asked Jennifer about the origin of her hair expertise, she didn't seem keen to discuss it. But after a bit more liquid coaxing, she told us she had taken a beauty-culture class in high school. Most hair shops hadn't wanted inexperienced teenagers working for them, so she took a job doing hair at a funeral home to obtain the required course credits. For a few moments, the only sound in that room was the timer. *Ding!*

"Dead people?" Danni choked back a coconut-rum spit-take. "No wonder you complained about us moving our heads too much when you cut our hair."

"Um...how did you...keep the head up?" I asked.

"The timer," Jennifer said.

Danni pressed on. "Did someone…hold it for you?"

"The timer," Jennifer said again.

"Come on, tell us!" I coaxed.

Jennifer held her hand up in protest. "Okay, okay, I used a neck block."

"*The timer!*"

After we were washed and blow-dried, the three of us stood in front of the bathroom mirror and surveyed our handiwork. Jennifer's streaky-blond mane had a strong resemblance to Van Halen's front man, David Lee Roth. She loved it. Danni gelled her platinum tips and called it her Tina Turner look. It was very chic with those exotic cheekbones of hers. Mine was not as successful. The top of my head was adorned with a pure-white crown of hair, and I was forced to wear bandanas to the office until I could find a hairdresser willing to fix it and to agree to an easy monthly payment plan.

Battle of the Bulge

There were many things about my body I was critical of, but it really came down to one thing—my butt. After three pregnancies, I could still boast a navel that was bikini worthy, and I wasn't overweight, but I would have liked a smaller tush. I agreed with Queen that fat-bottomed girls make the rockin' world go round, but they were singing about girls who were comfortable in their skin. I suffered from a condition known as "secretary's spread," due to the sedentary life style of my corporate vocation. My ego had taken also a hit when Hub was kind enough to point out I had a bit more flubber on the thigh since Peewee was born. I thought my new hairdo should slim me down, since it had worked so well for the dog. When I took her to the Poodle Parlor, she always came back looking ten pounds lighter. Unfortunately this Fido technique wasn't working for me, so either my new hairdresser was doing something wrong, or I'd have to get to work on slimming down.

Years ago women (and men) found a well-rounded female shape pleasing. But by the 1960s, curvy bodies became less vogue when Twiggy took to the fashion industry, and subtle pressures began for girls to be thin. At the time of my divorce, J. Lo hadn't yet hit the scene.

I was using my old Weight Watchers food scale as a planter in the kitchen, and it was time to dust the cobwebs from that exercise bike in the basement that I'd conscripted into duty as a laundry rack. The magazines in the staff room at work had many articles about body image, and I learned that listening to my body would bring an optimum balance of health and weight. So I listened. But the only thing I could hear were my thighs rubbing together as I walked. I should never wear cords.

Once again I enlisted Jennifer and Danni in my quest for change. They didn't need to lose weight either, but misery loves company, so they agreed to exercise along with me to get into better shape. Not having time or money to join a gym, we devised a plan to support each other through a nightly teleconference call that ensured we were all huffing and puffing with our Jane Fonda videos at exactly 9:00 p.m. After supper was over, laundry started, homework supervised, school notes signed, kids bathed and in bed, stories read, lunches made, and any current crisis dealt with, I'd get out my yoga mat and wait for the call. It was easy to recognize exercise time whenever I'd answer the phone and hear heavy breathing. I was dedicated and could have kept an obscene phone caller on the line without even noticing, while I concentrated on my obliques.

It was good to be doing more things for myself, and I began to feel I was taking charge of my situation. My life.

Even my nightly dream was changing. I dreamed the hospital called to tell me Hub had been in a serious accident in his new midlife-crisis sports car. He was asking to see me. I would arrive at the intensive care unit at 3:00 a.m., perfectly coifed and wearing Prada, and then sweep past D-Cup and Head Cheerleader to Hub's bedside. He would whisper his love and heartfelt apology for being such an incredible asshole before lapsing into unconsciousness. I alone would have the power to pull the plug.

5

TURN THE PAGE

Hi, Reader!

I'm glad you're still here. At a certain stage of the breakup, your social life had probably become a blur of wine and gal pals holding poor-me pity parties to moan about the ex factor: ex-husbands, ex-lovers, ex-money. I was tired of trying to hang on to the house and all the material things that had represented my life with Hub. I was tired of worrying about money. I was just plain tired. Were the red flags waving to end that chapter and move on?

Red Flags:

- You tell the guy at Recycle Depot the wine bottles are from your sister's wedding—again!
- Your ex pulls up in his new sports car to pick the kids up while you're under the hood of your old beater with a can of carburetor cleaner—again!

- Your nightly dinner conversation consists of "Sit down, eat your carrots, don't talk with your mouth full"—again!
- Your child support is late, and when you go to your ex's place, his girlfriend answers the door—again!
- You think a guy at the supermarket might be checking you out, but he's just fondling the melons—again!
- You want to get your groove back—again!

Games People Play

The quality of my new life revolved around Hub's sporadic support payments, and my weekends revolved around his sporadic visits with the children. If he picked them up, I could get all the housework and shopping done, plus squeeze in a little time for myself. If he didn't, I would do something fun with the kids, but there was little cleaning done and no "me time" at all. That often meant we had Mother Hubbard's cupboards, beds remained unmade, laundry joined the ranks of the great unwashed, and even the dog learned to dodge those sticky patches on the kitchen floor. Our recreational salvation came in the form of the community bowling alley. It housed an arcade where we could economically hone our skills at Whack-a-Mole and the Claw and a snack bar that served hamburgers as big as your head. While the kids were busy with their big-head burgers and favorite games, I would pursue a personal passion: perfecting my expertise on the shooting gallery. The face in my sights on that video game was always Hub's.

I was determined the kids were not going to miss out on celebrations and fun times just because their father wouldn't man up and pay his proper share of support. So my Visa started to pick up the slack, and soon a new tradition began in our home that was known for many years as the CCD, the credit card dinner.

The credit card dinner came about from two basic things—lack of cash and lack of desire to host another eardrum-piercing kid's birthday party at my house. It evolved to include lack of time, lack of energy, and lack of desire to cook. At a typical CCD, the kids took turns inviting one of their friends to join us—usually a brat. I always tried to choose a restaurant with the large, old-fashioned emergency lighting in the corner of the room. Those large bulbs proved to be the ultimate form of control. Upon entering the premises, I would inform the children that the lights were behavior detectors and that their actions would be monitored in a back room by the restaurant manager. Anyone who misbehaved would have their food taken away and be forced to sit quietly and watch the rest of us enjoy a lovely dessert.

If the weather was good, the CCD would be a take-out meal in the park. Outdoor control of unruly youngsters was more difficult since there was no emergency lighting to assist me. I told them if there was too much fooling around while eating, the seagulls would pick up the offending child and carry him away. This only worked with Peewee and his little guest. My two older kids had been on to me from the start. Middle Child had also figured out that the veal cutlets I served at dinner were breaded liver. He had taken great delight in watching his sister finish her last bite before blurting out his discovery. No more liver at our house.

Between a Rock and a Hard Place

As we approached the end of that school year, I began to worry about the looming increase in my childcare costs for the summer months. Hub was still in arrears with his support payments, but I was hesitant to call my lawyer about it. It was always difficult to hear his voice on the phone above the ringing of his cash register.

I suspected Hub's spotty payment record was part of a plan to put pressure on me to sell the house. He wanted his share of the equity but insisted it was to improve his financial situation, which would allow him to increase my support payments. Even Danni didn't have enough perfume to cover up the stench of that load of crap! I knew taking the kids out of their family home would be hard on them, but if the house was sold, I'd be able to buy a better car, pay the bills, and get back to some semblance of a normal life. I had two choices: stay broke or uproot and move. The rock and the hard place looked the same to me.

I had slashed the household expenses to the bone, and we'd been using single ply for months with little discernable savings. My salary was already stretched like spandex on the grade-six gym teacher's backside, so I developed a new system for dealing with my bills. I threw them on top of the refrigerator, where a paper mountain would build up until they started to slide off, and then I'd pay them in the order they hit the floor. Selling the house scared the hell out of me, but that fear was about more than just moving. It meant moving on. It was a sharp reality, but I had finally reached the breaking point.

Then Hub made me an offer. He would take the kids to live with him for the entire summer if I would commit to selling the house within the next six months. I was tired of a budget that never balanced and of passing off chopped Spam as ham salad. I agreed to sell.

After several frantic days of packing clothes, teddies, games, and swimsuits, the kids were ready to leave me for two whole months. They would only be across town, but I'd never been away from them for that long, and I wasn't sure how well Hub would cope. But he seemed genuine about having them, and that put me at ease. A little. As a last-minute gesture of goodwill, I even threw in a cheerfully wrapped gift to celebrate his birthday the following weekend. Nothing big—just a rectal thermometer I had never used. *Or had I?*

I waved good-bye to the kids, poured myself a glass of char-donnay, and sank into my comfy chair. Within a short time, I experienced two things that were foreign to me: complete silence and unlimited time to myself.

After the constant cacophony of my children and their band of friends, it was heaven. No yelling. No fighting. No sound of tin cups banging against the bars at dinnertime. I wallowed in the sheer pleasure of a quiet morning cup of coffee before work and came home to a house filled with nothing but the sound of the hamster wheel as I walked through the door at night. Only the dog was there to greet me with silent adoration. I could bask in the tranquility of an uninterrupted newspaper article or enjoy a television program of my own choice. The thrill of being in complete control of the channel changer for an entire evening made me a bit weepy. I made plans to join a book club, buy a new camera, and take a flower-arranging course. But most evenings would find me vegging in front of the TV. Then I experienced something else foreign—I was bored out of my skull!

It was time to call the girls.

Tonight We're Gonna Party like It's 1999!
Jennifer, Danni, and I had decided we should kick-start our non-existent social lives by going to the movies. But we always ended up doing more talking and less watching, and, for some reason, this annoyed the other patrons in the theater. So we switched to movie nights at home. Our first event was hosted by Danni and sponsored exclusively by tequila shooters. She had sold her divorce house and downsized to a new one in a subdivision with confusing street names that all sounded the same. Rose Street, Rose Avenue, Rose Ridge, Rose Close…Rose Ridge Close! The directions Danni had given me to Rose Terrace sounded confusing because they

were accurate. She said it would be easy to find her street because there was framework of a large house being built on the corner. After twenty minutes of circling the area, I was afraid construction would be completed, and I'd never find the address.

When I finally arrived at Danni's, she took my coat and showed me into the living room while detailing how much time and money she'd spent on the urban chic decor. I suspected she had enlisted one or two of the men she was dating to beat the furniture with chains to give it that stressed look. I had never seen so many shades of pink, but it was beautiful. The room had a relaxing glow from a large assortment of candles in different sizes and shapes.

Jennifer was settled on one of the oversized burgundy floor cushions with a makeshift bar in front of her. She poured each of us a drink, and Danni turned the TV to the Learning Channel. They were showing a vasectomy on *The Operation Show* that night. This was an important episode: the number one item on my bucket list was to witness a man in a hospital gown with his feet up in stirrups.

When we were satisfied the vasectomy patient was resting uncomfortably, Danni put *The Witches of Eastwick* into the VCR. After a few more tequilas, we began working some of the candles into our own voodoo dolls. Danni and I molded several crude wax stick figures, while Jennifer crafted a sculpture worthy of placement at Madame Tussauds of London. Her doll had six-pack abs and was anatomically correct—in every way.

"Hello, who is this well-endowed young man?" Danni's question was accompanied by an admiring wolf whistle.

"Let me introduce you to Mr. Paraffin Pete," Jennifer said and handed the figure to me.

After a brief inspection, I said, "I think his name should be Mr. Paraffin Goldberg."

I drove a huge safety pin into the top of my doll's soft little skull and thought of the recent headaches I'd had from fighting with Hub over the sale of our house.

"There, that ought to give him a good migraine. Did I do the right thing by agreeing to sell? Well, it's too late, and I have to find a way to stop obsessing about it all the time." My voice was rising, but my mood was sinking.

"I read somewhere that when you start thinking of your ex, you're supposed to visualize a large red stop sign," Jennifer said.

"That wouldn't help. I'd see Hub racing through that stop sign in his new car, into the path of an oncoming eighteen wheeler, and I'd be in the driver's seat."

"Visine eye drops can induce coma if ingested. You could invite him out for dinner and put a few drops in his wine," Danni added.

"Okay, so he's in a coma—then what do I do with him? And who would be paying for dinner?" I knew I was starting to sound unreasonable.

Jennifer refilled our glasses and set the bottle down in front of us. "You could load him into the car, take him out into the country, and dump him in a snowbank."

"It's July," I said.

"Okay, there's no snow. But don't give up on the Visine idea so quickly," Jennifer insisted. "Once you've dumped him, you could run over him with your car. I read a news story about a woman who did that a couple of years ago."

"I think they caught up to her when she tried it again with her second husband," I said. "But no worries—I'm *never* getting married again."

My voice had gone up another notch, so Danni patted my arm and said, "I heard about a guy living up north somewhere who'll do stuff like that for fifty dollars."

"Good price, but for now I can only dream that Hub will put himself into a Viagra-induced stupor and stay paralyzed and drooling for the rest of his life."

"Oh, I love that idea." Jennifer grinned. "He'd be completely aware of his surroundings but unable to move or speak."

Danni joined the enthusiasm. "Yeah, you could visit him at his nursing home and watch while some handsome, muscle-bound orderly gives him an enema."

"With his feet in stirrups," I added.

"Then you could make out with the orderly guy in the bed next to Hub's!" Jennifer's giggle was so infectious, the three of us sprawled out on the floor and laughed to the point of tears.

"I think I peed a bit," Jennifer squealed.

The ugliness of the mood I'd arrived with evaporated. Moving to a new place might not be so bad after all.

Danni put on her Cruella De Vil smile and poured three more shots. "It's been said the quickest way to a man's heart is through his stomach, but we know it's another part of the male anatomy."

"I'd rather have bamboo shoved under my fingernails than sleep with that man ever again!" I said and shoved a thumbtack into my little wax man's crotch.

"Calm down; you don't have to sleep with him, just cook him a nice meal, like chili with lots of beans. Lots and lots of beans." Danni had that wink-wink look she used when trying to be mysterious.

"So he farts himself to death?" I asked. "That wouldn't work. It's been dangerous for him to walk past an open flame for years, but he's still alive."

"No." Danni lowered her voice to a near whisper. "I've heard about some kind of beans that are poisonous."

"Let me guess—I can get them from a tall green guy named Jack." I laughed.

"They're castor beans." Jennifer said, "I planted them in pots on my balcony last year."

"And why did you do that?" Danni sounded suspicious.

"I used the plants for privacy from my creepy neighbor. They grew about five feet tall with large bushy leaves. The flower had a strange-looking seed pod with nasty prickles. That's the part that holds the poison bean."

"Figures—anything with a prick will hurt you," Danni said.

More laughter, more tequila.

I clapped my hands over my ears. "What would people think if they heard us talking like this?"

Jennifer flicked the air with her long, red fingernails. "Your Honor, our lips might have been moving, but Jose Cuervo was doing the talking."

Movie Mania

A week later we were at Rent Me Video, and all three of us had agreed on one thing. We would bypass romance and head straight to dramas and comedies. I nudged the girls toward the adult movie section at the back of the store and admitted I had never watched porn.

"What?" Danni's voice was a bit too loud.

"Shh…Hub asked me a couple of times, and I knew he watched porn at poker nights with the guys. But I guess I was just too insecure about myself. What about you?" I asked Danni.

"I used to ask Carl all the time, but he wasn't interested."

"But have you ever seen one?"

"Well…no, I haven't either," Danni admitted. "What about you, Jennifer?"

"Not interested," Jennifer said and walked away.

"Aw, come on," I whispered. "We keep saying we should be more adventurous. Let's rent a porno."

"I've never gone hang gliding, and I'm not interested in that either," Jennifer said. She picked up a movie without looking at it, paid for it, and walked out the door. Danni's perfect eyebrows arched even higher than usual as she stared after her.

I put my hand up. "Don't hassle her about it. You and I will get one tomorrow night. The kids are still at Hub's, so we can watch it at my place."

"I'm up for that. What did Jennifer rent for tonight?"

"I don't know. She just grabbed something. Hurry—she looks ready to leave without us!"

The next evening, I pulled my car up to the front of Rent Me, and Danni and I waited for the all customers to leave. After several long minutes, I said, "We'd better go in, or they'll think we're casing the joint and call the cops."

"You've been watching *The Sopranos* again, haven't you?" Danni said.

"Well, we can't just sit here; we look like criminals or idiots—or both!"

"Just get in there, and get the movie. Here's the money!" Danni pushed a few bills toward me.

I got out of the car, yanked open the passenger door, and pulled her out. "I don't care who pays, but you're coming in there with me!"

"I'll go in, but I'm not going to that section. It's full of pervs!"

"Don't be such a chicken sh...baby!"

People coming out of the store were starting to stare, and I began to have second thoughts about the whole thing.

"Look, the clerk is a woman about our age. We can ask her to go back there and get a movie for us," Danni suggested.

"Our age? She looks about twenty."

I grabbed Danni's coat sleeve and pulled her through the door with me. We looked like a couple of cats that had each swallowed a big fat yellow canary. Danni stepped behind me when I whispered our request to the young clerk.

The girl's face remained blank as she reached under the counter and brought out a movie. "How about *Oral Mania II?*"

"A sequel?" Danni protested. "They're always bad."

"Danni, these movies are all bad," I said as I grabbed the crumpled bills from her and handed them to Miss Deadpan.

I wasn't sure what the protocol was for watching an X-rated film, but I thought booze should play some part in it. Danni started the movie as I layered last year's Christmas liqueurs into a couple of martini glasses and handed one to her. "Madam, may I interest you in a Porntini?"

We raised our glasses in a toast, and I said, "Here's to being a little more daring."

"And here comes the delivery guy," Danni announced as she sipped her drink and pointed to the TV.

"He's not even good looking," I said. "I guess I had expected more of a Greek god."

"I doubt that we'll see any of those types in this movie. They're all working as models somewhere else."

As the movie continued, we complained about the poor quality of filming, bad lighting, and cheap set. Then we criticized the star's poor acting skills. I noticed there was no dialogue in that type of movie, so the repetitive action soon became boring.

I got up and went to the kitchen. "I'll make popcorn."

Danni offered to put the movie on pause.

"Don't bother."

"I'll give you a hand in there." Danni looked thoughtful as she propped her elbows on the counter. "Hey, did you think that redhead looked a bit like Jennifer?"

"What? No way—that movie must have been made years ago. Didn't you see that cheap and nasty old furniture? Jennifer wouldn't have been born yet."

"Hmm…or we could ask her if she's got a tattoo of a cobra between her boobs," Danni mused.

"Let's watch *The Witches of Eastwick*."

A Wolf in Wolf's Clothing

The girls and I avoided Rent Me Video for weeks, and with the end of summer, we had fallen back into our old routine of sitting around and complaining about life. We needed some fun. I had persuaded Hub to take the kids out on Halloween night, so we decided to treat ourselves to an evening out at Tricks Pub.

Halloween had always been a big deal at my house growing up. My mom would create amazing costumes for me and my siblings out of whatever she had in the house. I continued that tradition and always tried to make sure my kids had fun costumes. I have to admit it was much easier for me than it had been for my mother. I could find anything I needed in the charity shops and dollar stores. This year we'd have to make do with what was in the costume trunk. Middle Child wanted to be a mummy, but we didn't have enough gauze to wrap his whole body, so I added a few blotches of red food dye to his bandages, and he became an accident victim. My eye pencil created some acceptable-looking facial stitches, and a pillowcase fashioned into an arm sling completed his costume. Peewee had been wearing his clown outfit all day, and there was a large ketchup stain on the front. His father would have to deal with that. I had just finished braiding the orange yarn for my daughter's Raggedy Anne wig when Hub's car pulled up. The three kids grabbed their treat buckets and ran screaming out the door.

I poured a cup of coffee and was hoping for a few minutes in my comfy chair when the phone rang. The excited voice on the line didn't even bother with hello.

"What are you wearing?"

"Hello, Jennifer? Is this some kind of obscene phone call?"

"I meant, what costume are you wearing tonight?"

"Not sure. I haven't really had time to think about it."

"What? We're going out in less than an hour. Get ready!"

"I've got plenty of time; I can slap something together in fifteen minutes. What are you dressing as?"

"Sexy belly dancer, very sheer scarves."

"Yikes! And Danni, what's she wearing?"

"Sexy hula girl, very small coconut bra."

"Double yikes. You gals have set the bar pretty high. I guess I could wear my old hobo rags and be a sexy bum."

"Oh no, that's just wrong!"

When we got to Tricks Pub, "The Monster Mash" was blasting, and the place was swarming with people in the Halloween spirit. I picked my way through the throng and over to a corner where Dracula was serving a variety of bloody cocktails from his coffin-shaped bar. As I waited for the bartender to fix my plasma and Pernod, I watched some zombies and witches mingling around a big, sweaty baby sucking on a nipple stretched over the neck of a bottle of Coors Light. He was wearing a lacy bonnet and a sumo-style G-string diaper.

I had thrown together a Spanish señorita outfit, using my mother's satin wedding gown (sorry, Mom), some black lace, a plastic fan, and an excess of dark makeup. The costume didn't give me the same exposure as Jennifer and Danni, but I was wearing my new Heavenly Clouds antigravity push-up bra in an effort to turn the Spanish dancer into a bit of a vamp.

There was a lot of groping going on in the crowded bar, and I noticed some of the men dressed as women couldn't even keep their hands off their own boobs. Jennifer had warned me those guys often tried to use the ladies' washroom on Halloween night. She was right. I was brushing some fake cobwebs from the mirror to reinforce my beauty spot when a rather tall Red Riding Hood with frizzy black hair swaggered in, swinging a wicker basket on a rather muscular arm. Red's face was done up with huge eyelashes, big freckles, and rosy little-girl cheeks, but her clomping gait was like a Clydesdale.

"Hey, you can't come in here, no guys allowed!" I shouted.

Red kept on walking.

"How dare you?" I yelled.

The only response was the slam of a cubicle door.

I was heading back to our table to tell the girls about not-so-little Red Riding Hood when I felt a sharp pinch on my butt. I spun around to see a big, hairy wolf with huge claws and a lecherous smile. I recognized the grin belonged to Pete from my office.

"My, what big…eyes you have, little girl," he said, sliding a hairy arm around my waist and leering at my heavenly clouds.

"Good costume," I shouted over the music. "I see you're acting the part."

"Not as much as I'd like to," he slurred. "I'm here with my girlfriend. We're going to win the prize for best couple tonight; she's Little…and here she comes now. Hi, honey." Pete quickly removed his arm from my waist and said, "Let me introduce you."

"I think we met in the ladies room," I interrupted. "Sorry, gotta go."

I ducked out of that embarrassing introduction and through the crowd back to our table, but the girls weren't there. Danni was on the dance floor, draped over a buff-looking surfer dude, and

Jennifer had her jingling-coin scarves tangled around a swarthy Arabian knight. It was time for me to go home. I wanted to be sharp for parents' day at Middle Child's school in the morning and didn't want to wake up in a puddle of my own regret. He had invited his dad, and I hoped Hub wouldn't disappoint him.

Any semblance of my sexy señorita slid to the floor in a wrinkled heap as I fell into bed. In my dream, I stood under a streetlight wearing my mother's wedding gown and holding a violin case. As Hub came toward me out of the darkness, I opened the case and reached inside. At the bottom of the case lay a crumpled map to Middle Child's school. When I picked it up, Hub faded away.

The next morning, I arrived at the school early enough to get a good parking spot and made my way to Middle Child's classroom. There was no sign of Hub. The teacher had her head down, marking some papers when I walked in, but I recognized that frizzy black hair immediately.

"My…what a big classroom you have."

6

A MOVING EXPERIENCE

Dear Reader,

Have you heard the word "amicable" used in the same sentence as "divorce"? In my experience, most people bold enough to use that kind of language about their breakup are liars or living in La-La Land. I realized leaving my marital home was a necessary evil in the process of my divorce, but some red flags showed me the move wouldn't be easy.

Red Flags:

- You think you have enough newspaper and packing boxes. You don't.
- Your soon-to-be-ex-husband promises to look after the kids on moving day. He won't.

- You ask your neighbors to return the stepladder, measuring spoons, garden hose, electric fan, and the martini shaker they borrowed. They don't.
- That guy from work says he'll get the two hundred albums from his Columbia club record collection out of storage in your basement. He won't.
- People promise to help you move. They don't!

The Gloves Are Off!

All had been well in Hub Fantasyland when I stayed in our family home with our kids. He knew his assets were safe, and he still maintained ownership of them—all of them, including me. But his lust for a share of the equity from our home and my need for regular child support culminated in an agreement to sell the house. That was the last time we agreed on anything. When a buyer was found, Hub immediately became Lord of the Things. That's when the fighting over property began in earnest. Unfortunately, we weren't governed by any Marquis of Queensberry rules, which resulted in much wailing and gnashing of teeth.

Our lawyers were both chomping at the bit to handle the issue for us. That issue was our bank account. The only available funds we had were in the form of some jointly owned bonds I had purchased at my job through a payroll savings plan.

Dear readers, take my advice, and keep those stocks, bonds, and certificates in your own name. All of us should have a private bank account at a financial institution where our spouses do not conduct any business.

Common sense dictated that Hub and I should resolve the property settlement between the two of us to save time and legal costs. The problem with common sense is that it's not very common with divorcing couples. We tried sitting down over a cup of coffee, like two sane adults, to determine how things should be divided. We each made a list of what we expected to receive in the split. Our lists were almost identical—we both wanted the same things. Now, girls, be honest—did you find yourselves in the middle of a conversation that sounded something like this?

"Why the hell do you think you should have the _____ (please insert anything of value or something your ex wants)?"

"Because I paid for it!"

"*We* paid for it. I worked just as hard as you did, and I need it more than you do!"

"My dad gave it to me!"

"That old thing Pops wanted to get rid of? He was too lazy to take it to the dump, so he pawned it off on us—we replaced it years ago!"

I thought I was being fair when I offered Hub half the pots and pans, but he said he should have them all because I was a lousy cook and wouldn't need them. Once again, I found myself giving in to Hub's demands to keep the peace. But the negotiations completely broke down when he demanded the oven mitts I'd bought myself for Christmas. I finally stood my ground.

After it was all over, the only winners in our property settlement were the lawyers. My payroll savings bonds paid for all legal expenses. At the end of the month, I signed a raft of papers with our realtor and picked up the keys to have a look at one of his rental properties. I grabbed my poinsettia oven mitts, piled the kids into the car, and drove to number 36 Birch Street to start planning my new life.

"Mom, why are you wearing potholders to drive?"

A Sow's Ear

The potholder victory was sweet, but I didn't linger on it. My mind was climbing back over all the recent piles of garbage to a better time when Hub and I had bought our first house. I remember how excited we were to get there after a long day of jostling in the rusty old half ton. Tucked into the trees at the end of a mud-scored corduroy road, I caught my first glimpse of Sam Condie's old place— our new home in the country. But the closer we got, the smaller it became. Hub had made that spur-of-the-moment house purchase without consulting me and described it as cottage-style living. I wondered if I would ever appreciate it as much as Daniel Boone had. My husband opened the old screen door and left it hanging on one hinge as he carried me into the kitchen. The aroma of homemade apple pie quickly evaporated from my mind with one look at the old dinosaur McClary range.

"Oh my God, this place is a dump!"

Hub didn't reply as he pitched our earthly possessions through the front door without ceremony. Then he grabbed his hard hat, gave me a peck on the cheek, and headed back out to the old rust bucket. "Off to work in tin town. I'll be home in the morning. You should be done unpacking by then."

I hurried onto the step after him. "I thought you took the night off!" I hugged the old, gray sweater around my sagging shoulders and glared at his careless retreat.

Hub seemed unaware of the daggers I jabbed into his back as he jumped behind the wheel. Old Rusty started up with a cloud of blue smoke, and Hub gave an offhanded wave as they rattled off down the road. I looked back into the kitchen from the open doorway and shivered in spite of the heavy wool straightjacket around me. It would take a lot of work to make this sow's ear into the silk purse I had dreamed of.

Much to the relief of Daddy Longlegs and his large extended family, I gave up on the cleaning around midnight. I cleared away just enough space on the table to set down my coffee cup, along with a pen and paper for the next day's grocery list. Being alone in this remote place made me wish my mother hadn't been so eager to share her love of the Brothers Grimm with me. Some music would help, but I was afraid of adding more stress to the electrical octopus I had already created with the lamps and clocks. When I found a bottle of cooking sherry next to my box of old albums, the coffee-pot was sacrificed for the empowering words of Helen Reddy.

"I am woman!" I shouted into the inner recesses of the tiny house.

I reached to flip the record as a small shadow whispered away from me and across the floor into the corner. For a moment, I thought it was just too much Helen…or sherry. But then a glimpse of another fleeting little image—and then another. I slowly put down my glass, reached for the shopping list, and wrote "*mouse-traps*," followed by "*What the hell am I doing here?*"

During the next few days, I received a host of advice from Hub on how to deny entry to our unwanted little guests. I dutifully set about plugging the many cracks and crannies in the old walls with all manner of medium, from plaster and steel wool to tin foil. I also sprinkled a concoction of paprika and mothballs around the perimeter. This proved to be a lesson in futility, and I concluded we must have a strain of super mice attracted to a house that smells like a spicy old fur coat. No matter how many traps I put out each day, by the time Hub got home, they were all full. I could picture the loathsome little survivors gleefully scampering over the bodies of their fallen comrades and into my cupboards.

After a few weeks of driving twenty miles to the nearest grocery store, I'd become well versed in quantity purchases of anything in powdered form. I was busy complimenting myself on my superior shopping skills when I arrived home after one of my weekly trips. My arms were loaded with heavy bags, as I gave the stubborn old front door a kick and was greeted by a most peculiar sight. One of the mousetraps was spinning like a merry-go-round in the middle of the shiny, new lino floor Hub had installed in my kitchen the day before. To my horror, I realized it was being propelled by a mouse trying to free its tiny foot from the agony of the steel-jawed torture device I had placed under the stove that morning.

A half hour later, I was still on the front step with the grocery bags, finishing off the melting ice cream, when I heard a sound that was music to my ears. Hub was coming down the lane in our beautiful, rattily old Rusty. My knight had come to rescue me. I stood back and watched my brave hero through a hole in the screen door as he marched inside to rid my kitchen of the abomination. In an instant, the peaceful country air was shattered by my bloodcurdling scream when I saw his size-twelve work boot crashing down on the spinning trap and its wriggling contents.

"You bastard—you killed it!" I shrieked.

"Well...what did you expect?" Hub asked. "You wanted me to get rid of it."

"Not like that!" I screamed. "I hate them. But I hate killing them. I hate this house. And I hate living here!" I turned and ran sobbing into the bedroom and would have slammed the door if there had been one.

After a long cry, I splashed a little water on my face in the tiny bathroom and dragged myself back out to the kitchen. There was a large bouquet of ant-covered wildflowers on the table, and Hub was making a gallant attempt at lighting the old gas range to start supper. He handed me a mug with the last of the cooking sherry and pulled out a chair for me at the table.

The sting of tears on my cheek brought me back to reality as I turned onto Birch Street. All I could do now was shake off past thoughts of how different things should have been and get on with life. My newly rented home was at the far end of the street, and the closer I got, the smaller it became. I wondered if I had the energy to make another silk purse.

My Life in One Word

Sold! As soon as that sign was punched into our front yard, Bubba heaved his beefy belly over the back fence and fixed those bulbous eyes on my chest.

"I see you're moving—leaving anything behind?" He leered.

"Only the S and M equipment in the basement," I called over my shoulder and headed for the back door.

"Ah...well...er, why don't I come over now, and you can show me how..."

Slam!

Ten minutes later the old vulture from across the street waddled up my front step to join in on picking over the carcass of my crumbling life.

"You won't be needing those living room drapes where you're going, so I'll take them off your hands," she squawked.

"Where the hell do you think I'm going—prison?"

"Oh, I meant you won't have a nice, big window like this. Why don't I just come in and measure—"

Slam!

The following month rolled along, gathering tears, regrets, and myriad emotions into a big ball that stuck in my throat. When the mailman brought my final divorce decree, the ball moved from my throat and down into the pit of my stomach. It was time to start packing. A garage sale would have given me some much-needed extra cash, but I refused to give my neighbors the opportunity to probe through the remnants of my marriage. Peewee cried with me when the charity shop picked up his high chair and crib. His tears stopped after I told him he could start sleeping on the bottom bunk in Middle Child's room after we moved. Mine didn't.

My two best friends arrived with empty boxes and full wine bottles. Jennifer had arranged for her boss to help us move with his company's cube van. Danni said a guy she met at the gym would do the heaving lifting in exchange for a steak dinner. My budget said spaghetti, but I'd soon have my share of the house proceeds, so I splurged on T-bones for my little moving crew. Steaks would cost less than a moving company. Danni's Mr. Muscles proved to be an expert on the grill, and I emptied the contents of my fridge onto the table to accompany his culinary skills: a jar of brine with a couple of wrinkled pickles, two hardboiled eggs, and half a bottle of Bailey's. After the food disappeared, so did Danni and Mr. Muscles. Jennifer and I were left to finish the packing—and the wine.

The next morning, I was up with the sun and fully prepared for moving day. I was anxious for this next phase of my life and felt none of the trepidation I had expected. Coffee was brewing when the big white truck pulled up in front of my house, and little Jennifer jumped out from behind the wheel. I wondered why she was driving and how she could possibly reach the pedals.

"Where's your boss? He was supposed to help us." I could feel the ball in my stomach start to grow.

"He says he's got a sore back, but he's just a big lazy weenie."

Jennifer and I had the truck half-full of boxes, bikes, and lamps before Danni screeched up in her little red Miata. She was looking quite disheveled and not wearing any makeup. That was a bad sign. Danni didn't even take out the trash without her makeup on.

I smeared the sweat from my face with a grimy glove and glared at her. "Where's Mr. Muscles?"

"We had a fight, and he left." Danni looked down at the side-walk. "He's not at home, and he won't answer his phone."

The stomach ball got bigger. "Well, the next time you see him, reach down his throat, and get my steak back!"

I knew Danni thought I was angry at her, but what I really felt was the grip of fear bordering on panic. I had to maintain some semblance of control of the situation, so I did what I always do in crisis. I pushed my feelings down and piled them on top of the growing ball in my gut.

Danni didn't reply or try to defend her errant boyfriend. She went into the house, picked up one end of the couch, and put Jennifer at the other. As I watched the girls wrestle my furniture onto the truck, the ball slowly rose up from my stomach into my throat. The move was falling apart, and so was I.

I went down to the laundry room and stared at the washer and dryer for a long time. The three of us could never move those heavy appliances by ourselves, and it was too late to get a moving company on such short notice. The deadline for me to be out of the house was midnight. I had arranged to move on the last day possible to save an extra month's rent on the Birch Street property. The throat ball finally broke and spilled over.

I heard footsteps on the landing above me, so I pulled up the front of my grubby shirt and wiped my eyes. When I looked up, I saw a familiar pair of snakeskin boots coming down the stairs. Hub walked into the laundry room, pulling a beautiful, shiny moving dolly behind him. What a bastard.

Nightmare on Birch Street

With a final good-bye to our old house and the last load of treasures hauled from Eggy's hatchback, we were moved into our new home. I had two days left of a week's vacation to organize everything before going back to work. The kids were scheduled to stay at Hub's, but he had told them I needed help with unpacking, so he dropped them off and promised to pick them up the following weekend. I knew I wouldn't get much done with all three kids there anyway, so I gave Middle Child permission to invite a friend from the old neighborhood over for pizza. I thought having some fun with his buddies would be a good way for him to ease into his new surroundings.

Number 36 was a little bungalow on a beautiful street lined with large, silver birch trees. It was in an older part of town and hadn't been lived in for a while. I had described it to the girls as quaint. When they first saw it, Jennifer said it was cool, and Danni called it ancient. The old-fashioned design had no hallway, which put the bathroom directly off the kitchen. My bedroom was at the front of the house, through the living room, and had the only working telephone line. That didn't go over well with my daughter. A narrow, winding staircase led to an attic conversion with one large room. It was perfect for the boys, and I was foolish enough to let them start unpacking the boxes marked TOYS. When Middle Child opened the first box, his friend grabbed a Nerf basketball and hung the hoop over the closet door. The bunk beds weren't set up yet, so there was plenty of room for them to play. The game was on, but help with the unpacking was off. They were having fun in their new home, and that was more important, so I left them to it and went to help my daughter settle in.

The owner of the house had added a little bathroom in the basement and started another room next to it but left it unfinished.

We would all have to adjust to living in a much smaller place, so I convinced my daughter we could change that unfinished space into a bedroom for her with some innovative decorating. After a couple of quick trips to a nearby hardware store and a snack shop, we were ready to tackle the job. It was a good project for us to work on together, and it proved an excellent opportunity to bring out my daughter's creative side. We softened those bare cement walls with burlap, painted the floor, and put down the large multicolored rug I'd salvaged from the family room in our old house. Some funky orange-and-brown curtains hid the unfinished window frames, and she painted her old white little-girl furniture to match. The frilly bedspread and lampshades were replaced with a modern style, and a few dime-store picture frames turned her drawings and paintings into perfect artwork as a finishing touch. It was a place any young lady would be proud of, and she loved it. I offered to have a phone line put in her room if she unpacked all the boxes in the kitchen. I'd spend the next six months trying to locate the whereabouts of my cooking utensils, but it was worth it to see her so happy. The place started to look like home when Middle Child's cartoon creations of the Dippy Hippy were tacked onto the fridge door.

When my daughter was finished in the kitchen, we tried to put the bunk beds together, but I found there were no tools for the job. I hadn't thought to keep any when the house sold, and Hub cleaned out the garage. Women are supposed to be able to break into Fort Knox with a hairpin and fix cars with pantyhose, but I'd never been that kind of woman. We would have to make do with what we had. A nutcracker and high-heeled shoe eventually cobbled the beds together, but until they were reinforced, I decided that no one would use the top bunk. Middle Child would use the bottom bunk, and Peewee would have to sleep in my bed.

When the empty boxes began to outnumber the full ones, I decided it was time for dinner. At first, I thought our pizza delivery driver looked a bit like the guy from *Oral Mania*, but it must have been a hunger hallucination. After settling the battle over the last slice, I detected an odor in the room that wasn't just cheese. I needed to get out of my stinky clothes and get cleaned up, so I left the unpacking and headed for the bathroom.

That was when I first realized there was no shower, but the bathtub was a good size, and a nice, long soak would be a treat. As the tub filled, I noticed the cover for the heating vent was lifted about half an inch from the floor and waiting to trip me. I pushed and stomped on it, but couldn't force the cover back into place. Something was blocking the ductwork. Visions of the creature from the black lagoon came to mind as I gingerly reached down to pull out the offending blockage. A *Playboy*! I laughed at the thought of the previous tenant leaving his precious little secret behind. Then I noticed the magazine's date. It was the current month's issue and must have just been put there. Middle Child! Hmmm... what to do. I scanned the pile of boxes in the corner and ripped open the one marked BOOKS & STUFF. When I found an old *Vogue*, I carefully slid it down into the heat duct and replaced the cover. To this day, Middle Child and I have never spoken of this.

I peeled away my sweaty clothes and sank down to let the warm bubbles swallow me. It would have been heaven to have stayed in that tub for an hour or two, but there was a shitload of unpacking left and the kids to settle into their new bedrooms. Unfortunately, towels were the last thing on my mind before jumping into the tub, and my bathrobe was still lost somewhere in the moving shuffle. I stepped out of the bath and stood dripping on my wrinkled clothes while I rifled through a box marked TOWELS & STUFF. A miscellaneous assortment of junk dumped onto the floor...a set of egg cups, Christmas stationery, some pens, and two kitchen towels. I needed to get to my bedroom, so I dried off as best I could and struggled to cover up with the flimsy towels. But they were only big enough to cover one body part at a time—top or bottom. I debated putting my disgusting, wet clothes back on, but I could hear the boys were still jumping around with the basketball upstairs, so I decided to make a break for it. I held my breath, put the two little towels in front of me, with my bare backside to the wall, and tiptoed through the kitchen and living room. I slipped into my room, closed the door, and exhaled in a rush of relief. The towels dropped to the floor as I turned around to see Middle Child's friend sitting on the bed with the phone in his hand.

"I'm…I'm just calling my mom."

7

SUMMERTIME AND THE DATING AIN'T EASY

Hello Again,

Hooray, you stayed with me! This is where it starts to get interesting.

Are you single again? Are you feeling lonely and tired of doing everything on your own? Did that sound like a commercial for an introduction service? After my separation, there came a time when I answered yes to all of the above. That's when I started to think about dating again. Dating is the purgatory you go through when you want to meet someone for a relationship or just have some fun. There are all those exciting and terrifying "firsts" you have to go through all over again. The first date, first touch, first kiss, first...fart. Admit it—we've all kissed a few frogs along the way to meeting our Prince Charming, but the hard part is being able to tell which one is a true prince or which one is just a toad in prince clothing.

Red Flags of Dating:

- He invites you out for the best chicken dinner in town and takes you to KFC.
  Cheap!
- He displays a large crucifix on a gold chain over a Bart Simpson T-shirt with stinky pits.
  Reek!
- His dinner conversation includes the description of an excruciating ingrown toenail and the procedure to relieve his mother's impacted bowel.
  Geek!
- He tells you his BMW is in the shop but drives an old serial-killer-type van.
  Eeek!
- When he kisses you good night, he asks you to bring one of your girlfriends along on your next date.
  Freak!

On with the New

I started to enjoy the ease of managing a smaller place after the kids and I were settled into our little house on Birch Street. When I received my share of the proceeds from sale of our home, I paid off my credit card and bought a sporty little Toyota Celica. To say that car was impractical for someone with three kids was an understatement, but it was a beautiful black, and it was all mine. Relaxation became a new friend after I'd rid myself of the albatross of debt around my neck. I stopped chewing my nails at the end of each month and begging Hub for child support. His payments were still irregular, but he couldn't prey on my desperation anymore. Another added bonus was that my dreams had stopped.

The move had shortened my commute to and from work by almost an hour per day. It meant more time for the kids and the house and even a little for me. But by far the best thing was that not one person on the street knew me or anything about me—and nobody cared. No one was peering at me and my struggling life from behind closed curtains and whispering about me over back fences. No more Bubba next door or Bat-Woman across the street.

Bob Seger and I were singing "Against the Wind" on my drive home from work one Friday afternoon, and as I turned onto our beautiful, shaded street, I thought about the weekend ahead of me. At that moment, I realized the only company I was keeping was with coworkers, children, and women. I began to miss the male side of a conversation. Even the wrong side.

When I asked Danni to share the secret of her knack for dating, she said she used her feminine wiles. She certainly had her pick from a full man menu at her own Beefcake Café, and some of them looked pretty tasty. On Saturdays, when the kids were on playdates with friends, I'd stop by to drink coffee on her front porch and watch the construction site across the street. It proved to be worthwhile entertainment. Danni would make a grand exit from the garage with the lawnmower, just as the workers were sitting down with their lunch buckets. That mower never seemed to start without the help from at least two of them, but she made it clear the hard hats from across the street were only there to mow the lawn. Danni had recently started to talk about having another child and assured me her serial dating days were over. Courting had become a kind of distilling process for her to find the purest designer genes for a baby. Perhaps a castoff from her testosterone lawn-cutting smorg might be interested in me. I'd have to get myself some of those wiles she was talking about.

One sultry Saturday, Danni's seduction kit included pink Daisy Dukes and matching pumps. The outfit was a little over the top, but what the heck—the grass was getting cut. She had dropped a not-so-subtle hint about my choice of man-watching wear when I got to her house that day. After a few maternal pats on the shoulder, she told me my T-shirt was a boner shrinker. I took offense to that. I had bought the shirt just after Hub left, and I thought it was pretty cute. It was a perfect fit and had the most adorable little smiling goldfish on the front. Danni explained it wasn't the style or fit she was concerned about. It was the speech bubble above the shiny fish head that read, "A Woman without a Man Is like a Fish without a Bicycle."

I had no time to stay and ogle at construction workers or quibble over man-watching fashion that morning. Jennifer was coming to my house with tools to put the boys' bunk beds together. I drained the last of my coffee and jumped into my Celica, leaving Danni striking a come-hither pose over a garden rake. Hub had promised to fix those beds, but after three weeks, Peewee was still sleeping with me. I was getting tired of waking up with cracker crumbs and banana peels. Since he'd been sprung from behind the bars of his crib, Peewee had started getting up at night to forage the cupboards and was bringing his treasures back to bed. I was too exhausted to wake up when he crawled out of bed and only became aware of his habit after finding cookies under his pillow and a half-eaten apple digging into my back.

I picked the kids up on my way home, and when I parked in front of the house, Jennifer was walking up the steps with a battered old toolbox and a bag of Krispy Kremes.

"Wow, that thing has seen better days," I said, pointing to the dented red box.

"My stepdad gave this to me a long time ago. He always made sure I had tools, so I didn't have to depend on a guy for anything."

"Good advice; I could have used that a few years ago. I depended on a guy that wasn't dependable."

The kids elbowed each other from the car and started circling Jennifer and the donuts like birds of prey.

"Step away from the guest!" I took the donuts and handed one to each of the little vultures. Then I poured three glasses of milk and turned to Jennifer. "You know, I'm starting to think about dating again."

She picked up a chocolate glaze and gave me one of her measured looks. "About time."

Armed with Krispy Kremes, wrenches, and screwdrivers, we spent the next half hour tackling the wobbly beds. When we put the tools down, I licked the icing from my fingers, climbed onto the top bunk, and bounced around a bit to test our handiwork. The beds stood firm.

I was anxious to start waking up to fresh sheets without any of Peewee's food residue, so I asked Jennifer to help me strip my bed for the laundry. We each grabbed a corner of the unmade bedclothes and pulled. As the pile of jumbled sheets peeled away from the mattress, a large carrot flew through the air and landed on the floor at our feet.

Jennifer leveled those brown eyes at me. "Oh yeah, its time you started dating again."

Lookin' for Love in All the Wrong Places

We've all heard that you can meet the man of your dreams at the supermarket, but no Prince Charming was ever going to look twice at a woman whose shopping cart was piled with reduced-price stickers and three kids in tow. Marriage didn't seem to work for me, so I wasn't interested in anything permanent. I just wanted to have some male company and maybe a little fun. Tell me, girls, where does a single woman with a ton of baggage find a guy like that? I started to take stock of the eligible men at my office. It didn't take me long to realize that men on their way up the corporate ladder were only interested in stepping on and over me to get to the top. That wasn't too difficult for them, since I was only able to climb that ladder with one hand on the rungs while the other struggled to keep a grip on my kids, my bills, my house, my car... my life.

Jennifer had also started to complain about the lack of eligible men in her life, so we tried writing a joint ad for a dating service. It sounded too much like the lyrics of a third-rate country song, so we scrapped it. But it gave us an idea. We called Danni, and, with no fear or good judgment holding us back, we decided to take a giant step out of our comfort zone to try something completely different. A country bar.

Girls, I hate country music and can only two-step if I lead, but Happy Jack's was a new place without any peanut shells or straw on the floor. I have to admit I enjoyed the daggered looks from the boot-scootin' cowgirls as I walked in wearing four-inch sling backs, a black pencil skirt, and a creamy satin blouse. Unfortunately that heady feeling was short lived when I realized I was missing one of my new stick-on shoulder pads. As Danni ordered drinks, I ducked my head under the table and scanned the floor in search of the wayward foam rubber. Jennifer tapped my shoulder and discretely advised me she'd located the wardrobe enhancement. It had merely moved to the middle of my back, and after a few adjustments in the gals' room, my shoulders were once again as imposing as Stallone's. For the rest of the evening, I was known as Quasimodo.

We all know that a girl can't be in the ladies' room in front of a large mirror and cruel, unforgiving lighting without doing a few touch-ups. So I quickly dabbed on some Luscious Lips and pulled out the Big Guns mascara. In my haste, I stabbed the wand directly into my left eye, and a familiar cycle began. The eye waters, you fix the mascara, the eye waters, you fix mascara…and repeat. Danni said I shouldn't worry, as it gave me a mysterious dewy-eyed look. I began to think she might have been right when a handsome throwback to the seventies swaggered over.

"Wanna dance? Saw you winkin' at me," he drawled.

"No, my eye—hell yeah, I wanna dance!"

When Mullet Man walked me back to the table, he asked for my phone number, and I explained I don't give my number to strangers.

"Okay, then I guess I won't be offering you any candy," he said as he walked away.

"What grade are you in at middle school?" Danni blasted.

Her voice was raised because of the loud music, but I felt chastised, and it made me ashamed of how childish my response to Mullet Man had sounded. I was out of my depth, floundering back into the uncharted waters of dating again. I wasn't ready to jump into the deep end—just wanted to dip my toe in and paddle around a little.

My mood was beginning to sink when Jennifer marched over, clutching the bulging bicep of a red lumberjack shirtsleeve. She'd been invited to a keg party in the country and insisted Danni and I go with her. I hesitated, but the kids were with Hub for the weekend, and an outdoor party sounded like fun. It also might open a door for us to find love or lust—whichever came first. We chipped in for a large case of beer, jumped into my car, and followed Mr. Lumberjack's half ton out of town until he stopped at a clearing in the trees. More than a dozen cars, trucks, and motorcycles were parked by a stream in a picture-book-perfect setting. The party was in full swing, with a large group of people around several picnic tables loaded with bottles, cans, and red plastic cups. The group looked like a good mix, with a few nuts and kooks thrown in. I recognized several of Hub's golfing buddies in a tight little circle. They had been my friends, too, before the divorce, so we exchanged awkward, halfhearted waves. Their wives looked the other way.

Two large speakers dangled from overhead tree branches and were blasting a tune with lyrics about a man with incomplete genitalia on his way to a rodeo. Everyone was singing along and seemed to know all the words. A patch of meadow under a small tree had been smoothed down to hard-packed dirt by a horde of feet and served as a dance floor. The two young ladies occupying the floor looked a lot like a couple of the incompetent babysitters I'd hired during my evening college classes when Hub stopped sharing childcare responsibilities. I watched them gyrate around the tree, practicing for their future pole-dancing vocations. Steppenwolf seized hold of the speakers, and when "Born to Be Wild" hit the airwaves, the pole dancers were set adrift by a sea of leather as the bikers took over the dirt floor.

Mr. Lumberjack opened our case of beer, gave us each one, and put the remaining bottles in a big cooler with the others— many others. Then he lifted a cardboard box from the front seat of his truck, flipped down the tailgate, and turned it into an in-stant shooter bar with an impressive variety of alcoholic beverage choices. Soon Jennifer was at his side, demonstrating her mixology skills to a growing crowd of admirers, who were more than willing to part with their cash.

Up to that point, the highlight of the evening had been when an old biker showed us how he could pick a fly off the picnic table by clapping his hands in the air above it.

He was so darn good at it that we were soon all trying it… and I caught one! That accomplishment resulted in boisterous ac-colades from the bikers. The fly wasn't dead and flew away when I opened my hands, but I insisted I'd made his beady little eyes water. A huge bonfire warmed the evening air, and the tree-stump seating around it looked appealing, from the height of my stilettos. A whiff of something cooking prodded my stomach into a low growl and reminded me I hadn't eaten since breakfast. The heels of my flimsy shoes stabbed into the grass as my nose followed the tempting aroma to Mullet Man, roasting a hot dog on the end of a stick.

He nodded. "Wa'sup?"

I giggled. The beer or the heady fragrance of that hot dog in the fire made me start seeing Mullet Man in a different light. Even the prison-quality tattoo on his forearm was more appealing. It looked like a black panther or a closed fist, depending on the re-flection of the flames. I watched as he twirled the stick around and around in one hand with great expertise. Then I discreetly pointed out he had neglected to remove the plastic wrapper from the hot dog. Mullet immediately pulled it from the flames but seemed quite pleased with the results…and ate it.

"Gives it a nice crunchy coating. Want one?"

It had been a long time since a man had cooked dinner for me, but I had envisioned it would be somewhat different and declined the offer.

As I scanned the crowd for Danni, I noticed Hub had joined his friends by the fire and had his arm around one of the wives. The sight of him draped over that woman triggered ugly memories of his past behavior, whenever we had been in mixed company. My party mood was replaced with the old, rotten feelings of hurt, anger, and betrayal—the ones I thought I'd left behind with Bubba and Bat-Woman, in the old neighborhood. I debated leaving but decided that would be childish. I was there first!

Danni was trolling a group of young cowboys beside a large pile of freshly cut trees at the bonfire with her potential-boyfriend net, so I made my way over there to see what she'd caught. The boys said they were in charge of the logs, but by the look of the bulges in their jeans, it was Danni who controlled the wood. The longest pair of Wranglers flashed a smile in my direction that would do any orthodontist proud. He popped the tops from two cans of Bud and handed one to me. I managed to stop short of fluttering my eyelashes but tried to look coy as I took a dainty sip of my beer. Wrangler drained his can in one gulp and threw it into the fire. My approving smile at his manly gesture prompted him to grab for another beer, but he picked up a can of OFF bug spray by mistake. Wrangler laughed like a braying donkey, flashed those pearly whites again, and tossed the repellent into the flames beside his empty beer can. I stopped smiling.

"Danni, we have to leave—now!" I snapped the spaghetti strap on her bare shoulder.

"What—now, with all this beautiful scenery?" Her eyes drooled over the cowboys.

"Some idiot just threw an OFF can into the fire!"

"Threw a can off what?" Danni shrugged my hand away.

"OFF! The bug spray. Listen to me. That's dangerous." My voice began to rise, like it always did when I was frightened or nervous or mad. "Those warnings are there for a reason." I was starting to sound as though I'd sucked on a helium balloon.

"Yeah, to scare kids, not grownups. Can't you stop being a mom for one evening? I bet you could quote the warning label from that can from memory."

I slipped out of my shoes and backed away from the fire. *Do not use near heat, sparks, or open flame.*

The beer grew warm in my hand as I fixated on the bright—orange can snuggled down in the glowing embers. Someone let out a loud shriek, and I saw smoke spiral up from the back tire of a motorcycle that had been parked too close to the flames. While we watched the owner push his bike to safer ground, I heard a sharp hissing sound from the fire pit. My mouth opened in a muted scream as the little orange missile came roaring out of the fire propelled by a long, bright tail of sparks. It smashed right into the middle of Hub's chest!

I had a perfect view as the force of that OFF bomb knocked my ex-husband straight back off the tree stump he was sitting on. He hit the ground with a loud thud, and everyone rushed over as Hub lay in the dirt writhing for air. Wrangler put his arm around my shoulder and propelled us through the crowd to get a closer look at the helpless figure curled up on the ground. That donkey bray reached new heights as Wrangler claimed bragging rights to the bug-spray prank. Many of the partiers found this hilarious and walked him over to the tailgate bar for a round of congratulatory shooters.

Hub's watery eyes looked up at me as he clutched his chest and rasped, "My heart." I turned and walked toward my car. *What heart?*

Dirty Deeds

Another weekend had arrived, and once again I was alone and singing along with Whitesnake. I was more than a little pleased when Danni called to say her date had canceled at the last minute, and she suggested we go to Tricks for a quiet drink. We hadn't seen much of her since her hook-up with one of the guys at the keg party. I thought he was a real knuckle-dragger and that she could do better, but I had to admit he was pretty darn cute. Danni knew he wasn't the brightest and was much too young for her, but he sure looked good on her arm. Jennifer planned to walk over and meet us at Tricks after she finished work, so I was ready and out the door in less than half an hour.

Danni and I found Jennifer sitting at a table with three bottles of beer in front of her when we walked into the pub. We hadn't planned to stay long, but the KISS cover band was in full costume, so I was soon at the bar for a second round of beer and a couple of shots for the girls. On my way back to our table, I noticed a familiar face deep in conversation with the cleavage of some sweet young thing.

"Danni, isn't that the knuckle-dragger who broke a date with you tonight?"

"Where?" Danni's head did a 360 around the room. "And don't call him that!"

"I'm going over there to find out what the hell he's doing here with little Miss Sweet Thing when he's supposed to be working!" Danni's voice threatened to drown out the band. So much for a quiet drink.

"No way!" Jennifer grabbed her arm. "Let's just follow her into the ladies room and scare the shi—"

"We're not following anyone anywhere," I interrupted. "We all know where that type of thing will end—handbags at dawn!"

Jennifer dismissed me with a wave of a tiny manicured hand. "Just give him your signature go-to-hell look. He'll soon come running over here. Or poke a hole in his tire."

"A puncture is worth a thousand words." Danni cackled.

That crazy laugh made me realize she was at the point of intoxication where her tongue had become disengaged from her brain, and we should leave.

In the parking lot, Danni pointed to a half ton with a bumper sticker: Does This Truck Make My Neck Look Red? "Oh, please just let me do something to his precious truck," she pleaded.

"Hang your panties on the side mirror, and let's get out of here," Jennifer suggested.

"That would be a great idea if I was wearing underwear," Danni replied and turned toward me.

I stepped back. "Don't look at me!"

"Oh, please don't tell me you're still wearing those tighty-whities." Danni gave a little toss of her perfect hair.

"Well…until I meet someone, I guess." I tried not to sound defensive.

Jennifer finally agreed she would sacrifice her thong for the worthy cause of revenge. After the underwear was in place, Danni opened her purse and took out a minipad. "Who's got a pen?"

I found a Sharpie at the bottom of my bag, and Danni scratched a few words onto the Stayfree. Then she peeled off the paper backing and stuck it to the windshield of the truck. MEET ME AT MY PAD—NOW!

The sky was clear and bursting with a million tiny lights when we got to Danni's house. She grabbed a six-pack from the fridge and brought it out onto the front step. It was a shame she was too pissed off to enjoy the cool breeze and cold beer with Jennifer and me. There was one beer left when Knuckle-Dragger's truck pulled up in a cloud of blue smoke. He sauntered over to the step wearing his sorry-little-boy look for Danni.

"Aw, come on, honey, she's just my cousin," he whined.

"Yeah, kissin' cousin! How stupid do you think I am?"

"Well, not that stupid. But really, she's my cousin's friend, and I wasn't even there with her," he said and grabbed the last beer from the case. "She sat down in the chair next to me, and I was just holding it until her boyfriend got there."

"Holding what?" Danni screeched.

The couple moved their fight inside, while Jennifer and I decided to make the most of what was left of the starry sky and take a walk to the park at the end of the street.

"We both know where this will end," I said.

"Yep. In the bedroom."

A Real Date

One of the perks of my shortened commute to the office from Birch Street was the extra time I had to go home on my lunch break. It gave me the opportunity to get a start on what lay ahead after work. I would put dinner in the slow cooker, make beds, tidy up, and even vacuum a bit. The house became a much more welcoming place to come home to at the end of each day, and I loved the break from the office. Sunshine could make any manic Monday better, even through the windshield of my car. My new routine was working well, until the day I rushed back to work to find a large vehicle squeezed into my reserved parking stall. I was late and knew it would be difficult to find alternate parking nearby, so I needed to have the humongous thing towed. I stopped my car behind the black monster and proceeded to write down the plate number.

"No, please…sorry, sorry!" A man ran up to me, extended his hand, and began what probably would have sounded like a sincere apology to anyone other than me.

I was mad. This wasn't the first time I'd had my parking spot stolen, and I unleashed a litany of choice irreverence at him. He continued to apologize as he moved his vehicle, but I was done talking. I screeched my car into place and ran into the building without a reply.

When I got to work the next morning, the parking thief was waiting by the door, with a rose, a sheepish look, and an invitation to lunch. That was when I noticed he was tall, slightly gray, and quite good looking. The decision between going home to do housework or being treated to lunch was a no-brainer. I agreed to meet him next door at Bea's Bistro at twelve. It was hard to concentrate on work that morning, and I had called Danni so many times for advice she stopped answering her phone. Just before noon, I made a pit stop at the washroom mirror to check for any cosmetic faux pas and set off for my date. Was it a date?

After we introduced ourselves at Bea's, I realized Tom had a mustache. I'm not a big fan of the 'stache, but this one was well trimmed and attached to a guy who held my chair for me when we reached our table. The pear and avocado salad was delicious, and I was pleased with how relaxed our conversation was. I learned Tom was the principal of a school in a small community about an hour's drive from the city. He was divorced, with custody of an eleven-year-old daughter. When he told me he coached her soccer team, I forgave him for driving that large SUV.

Pinch me! Could this be real…a polite, good-looking guy who likes kids is interested in me? I sprinkled a few shards of my fractured life into the conversation, with caution and without revealing too much of the wreckage. This was to keep him from screaming into the street and back to the safety of his rural roots. My dear reader, there are many other reasons to be cautious about what we share with some-one we have just met. We don't know what people will do with the in-formation we give them, and some of the dregs of society are masters at ferreting out any indiscreet morsel to use as a tool of manipulation.

My lunch hour was over much too soon but not before we exchanged numbers. Tom promised to call me on the weekend, and I had three whole days to wait. By Sunday afternoon, my nails were chewed to the quick, and Danni told me if I promised to stop calling her, she would come over after dinner to stare at the telephone with me.

I met her at the door. "Maybe I should call him. I should call him, shouldn't I?"

"Hello to you, too, and, no, you should not call him!" Danni's emphatic response quashed that idea in a big hurry.

I popped corn and rolled sleeping bags out onto the living room rug for the kids to watch the umpteenth showing of *Dr. Doolittle*. Danni and I took our coffee cups to the bedroom and made ourselves comfy on the floor with the phone between us.

"What if he's waiting for me to call him?" I knew that was a reach.

"So what? Let him wait. You don't even know this guy."

"But I felt a connection with him. He has a kind of an animal magnetism."

"Yeah, a crouching tiger, hidden pervert."

Danni had been watching a lot of martial arts films with Knuckle-Dragger, so I ignored that remark. I knew she was wrong about Tom.

"Look, this is the first guy you've met since your divorce, and he won't be the last. The phone isn't ringing, is it?"

We both jumped as the brassy ringtone cut between us.

"Hello?" I squeaked.

"Hi, it's Tom."

By the time I put the phone down, Danni was gone, the kids were asleep, and I had a date for the theater the following Saturday night.

At the end of a long week, I stood in front of the bedroom mirror in my underwear and shivered. Jennifer pulled hangers out of my closet and tossed clothes onto two piles. The smaller was dubbed "keep," and the large one "burn." Some of the outfits she put together looked rather funky, but they weren't really my style. I kept going back to the creamy satin shirt and black pencil skirt.

"Not that again; you need to get away from old faithful and into something different." She handed me a calf-length paisley skirt with a skinny black turtleneck. "You can wear my new boots and pair it with this fabulous silver jewelry I just happen to have in my purse." Jennifer looked quite pleased with herself.

"Danni told me I should meet Tom at the theater, instead of having him pick me up at home, but I don't think that's necessary. He's a perfect gentleman."

Jennifer weighed my words with a long look. "Meet him there. They might find bodies in his basement someday, and I don't want one of them to be yours."

Tom let out a soft whistle of approval when I walked into the theater lobby just before curtain time. Jennifer had done well. The play was *No Sex Please, We're British*, and it was good to share a laugh with a man again. Hub liked comedy but would never have taken me to live theater, even if the title had the word "sex" in it. At intermission, I scanned the audience for any familiar faces. I would have loved for Bat-Woman or Mary Hard-Faced-Bitch to see me on Tom's arm. He held my hand through the second half of the play and gave it a little squeeze when he laughed.

We shuffled out with the crowd after the final curtain, and Tom suggested a drink at the Theater Bar nearby.

"Great idea; my treat." I thought it only fair that I pay for drinks, since he had picked up the show tickets.

As Tom helped me with my coat, Hub and a distinguished-looking older woman stepped in front of us.

"Hello," I said and made no effort to control my grin.

"Hi," Hub mumbled and moved on.

I turned to Tom. "My ex."

"She's a bit long in the tooth for him, isn't she?"

"Hmm...probably has money. He likes money."

I watched Hub escort old Snaggletooth out the door and smiled. Nothing could spoil my evening.

When Tom ordered a second drink, I peeked at my watch and reminded him he had a long drive home ahead of him. He didn't seem concerned, and I kicked myself for reverting back to the same old role I'd played as the responsible half of my failed marriage.

Our walk back to the theater parking lot was a slow, arm-in-arm stroll to heaven. His kiss at my car door made me tingle, and it wasn't just the mustache. Tom suggested we get in and listen to some music, but I wasn't so out of touch with the whole man/woman thing not to know what that meant. I looked at my watch and told him he should be heading home.

His finger touched the tip of my nose, and he whispered, "I could go back in the morning. My daughter is at her mother's for the weekend."

"Sorry, my kids are at home, and I think we have all that ahead of us."

"Okay." He grinned and pulled himself away from me. "I'll call you next week."

He didn't.

"What did I do wrong?" I waved my arms as I paced around Danni's gleaming chrome kitchen. "He didn't like my outfit. I knew that sweater looked too slutty."

"Stop!" Danni grabbed my shoulders and steered me to a chair. "This has nothing to do with what you were wearing. And there isn't a single female garment in the world that's too slutty for any guy."

I forced a weak laugh.

She put her face close to mine. "He hasn't called because the old horn dog was expecting to get laid on your first date, and he's pissed off because it didn't happen."

"But he brought me a rose, and he likes kids, and we laughed, and he held my hand, and…"

Danni's tone softened, "Okay, maybe you should call him and let him explain. You deserve that much. He might have lost your number or died in a fiery crash," she added.

"Hey, don't talk like that!"

"Sorry. I just have an uneasy feeling about the guy. There was something sleazy about him."

"No, I'm not going to call him. Tom knows where I work. He could park in my spot again if he wanted to see me." The feeble joke was a poor attempt to cover my anxiety of why I hadn't heard from him.

Danni was right. I had put too much stock in my first romantic encounter, and she was also right that Tom wouldn't be the last. But she was wrong about him. In my heart, I knew he was a nice guy, and his motive for not calling had nothing to do with sex—or the lack of it.

Fun with Dick and James

In the following weeks, I was determined to put Tom out of my mind and concentrate on my family and work. The house was cleaner than it had been since we'd moved in, and I had started to exercise again. If the kids were at Hub's on weekends, Jennifer would come over Saturday night to play Trivial Pursuit while I did housework. We had revamped the game by getting rid of the board so I could continue with the cleaning and laundry. I had the trivia cards on the table and ironing board set up when Jennifer got to my house after dinner.

"Get dressed. We're not playing tonight," she said and packed up the game. "We're going dancing at Tricks. You know what they say. The best way to get over a man is to get under another one. A one-night stand wouldn't hurt you."

She propelled me into the bedroom and proceeded to pants me out of my baggy sweats.

"I can dress myself, thank you very much," I protested. "And I'm not interested in a relationship like that!"

Now, girls, I'm not going to get into all the pros and cons of the one-night stand, but be careful to recognize it for what it is. The label speaks for itself. One night. It is not a relationship.

I was still licking the open wound from my first unsuccessful foray into dating, but the music and uplifting atmosphere at Tricks soon eliminated any lingering apprehension. I looked at it like breaking in a new bra: a little uncomfortable at first, but possible with proper support.

That night Jennifer and I were at the pub to have fun and not think about our clothes, hair, makeup, or dating. For most of the evening, we danced with two men who looked like they'd just stepped off the cover of *GQ* magazine. Richard had such an infectious dry wit that I couldn't hold his good looks against him. Jim was only interested in anything and everything Jennifer. So that left me trying not to stare at the green flecks in Richard's beautiful hazel eyes. We wanted to make an early night of it, so the boys invited us to join them at the shooter bar for one last drink before we left. I tend to stay away from shots of any kind, since they have a habit of making me drunk, but one wouldn't hurt.

The hundred-watt bulb above the front door was a spotlight, glaring down at my little stumble on the top step. I was shit faced! Jennifer grabbed my key, helped me to my room, and let me belly flop onto the bed. She put a glass of water with two aspirin on the nightstand and bucket beside the bed. After she left, I thought about all those nasty Prairie Fire shooters, and my stomach rolled, but I could not be sick. There was no one to hold my hair back.

A ring, ring, ringing exploded inside my head, and the blurry red dial on my bedside clock looked like 3:20 a.m. "Hello?" I croaked into the phone. My mouth tasted like the inside of a football player's jock strap.

"Hi, is this Lois?"

"No Lois here; wrong number." I hung up and turned my back on the noisy intruder. *Ring!*

I grabbed the receiver. "What the?"

"Hi, again…um, don't hang up. It's Tom."

I dropped the receiver and pushed the telephone to the floor in a clanging heap.

A fucking booty call, and he couldn't even remember my name. Danni had been right about Tom. She'd been right about everything. I reached for the bucket.

8

THE UGLY, THE BAD, AND THE GOOD

Okay, girls, now it's your turn!

I paved the rocky road of dating after divorce with plenty of ice cream, wine, laughter, and tears shared with my besties. Along the way, I met many women who still harbored leftover demons from their experiences. This chapter gives them a voice to exorcise those dating devils. Here are their stories.

The Girls Speak

Lori: I had a crush on the cable guy who worked in my building, so I spent some hard-earned cash on tickets to a Matchbox Twenty concert and invited him to come with me. He accepted with genuine enthusiasm, and I even agreed to pick him up. I was in a great mood when we arrived at the concert—my favorite band and a date with my favorite crush! Cable Guy ignored me through the entire show. He didn't speak to me on the drive back to his place, either, but when we got there, he asked me in for coffee. He probably expected to get laid. I accepted the invitation to prove that he wasn't going to!

Andrea: I thought I'd hit the jackpot when I started seeing an elementary-school teacher. Finally, a guy with brains! We had dinner at his apartment, and, after dessert, he took me to the den and showed me his extensive collection of *Juggs* magazines. He was quick to point out the skin publications were displayed in chronological order on a custom-made stand. What kind of guy thinks something like that would impress a girl on a first date? Likely the kind that holds his girlfriend's head under the covers when he farts. I didn't stick around to find out.

Elizabeth: Some women feel they have a "best before" date stamped on their butts—especially if there's a little cellulite in the area. I was still trying to get over that type of poor body image when my new relationship progressed to the intimacy stage. I made sure the bedroom was always dark, but after a while, Matt began to tease me about the lack of boudoir lighting. A sense of humor has always been important to me in any relationship, so I bought him a pack of glow-in-the-dark condoms at a novelty shop. I knew this was the man for me when he proceeded to model one for me that night and do a cheeky little dance around the darkened room with a pair of my underwear on his head. We both laughed, until he began to experience an uncomfortable (and unsightly) reaction to the luminous prophylactic. After we read the warning label, I was the only one laughing.

Josie: After leaving a marriage because of my husband's alcoholism, I was happy to meet a tall, distinguished-looking gentleman who didn't drink. I told him I enjoyed a glass of wine with a good meal or a beer on a hot day, and he seemed to be all right with that. I was confident we would have none of the relationship problems that often accompany alcoholism: money, infidelity, abuse—the list goes on.

The first red flag was at my annual staff picnic when I reached for a second beer. He became sullen, and his conversation was stilted. The second was at his daughter's wedding. When I refilled my wine glass at the reception, he left me at our table with his ex-wife for more than an hour while he sat with other guests. After the bride and groom had left on their honeymoon, we had a raging fight, and I told him it was obvious he didn't want me to drink. He denied it. Since I thought I had a future with this man, and alcohol wasn't an important part of my life, I gave up my dinner wine and cold brew when we were together. Then I quit having an occasional drink with friends and coworkers.

By our first anniversary, he had bought his and hers matching tracksuits and started making plans for me to move into his house. When I told him I needed time to give serious thought to such a big decision, he started pacing the room and didn't speak for a long time. Then he announced he was cutting down on caffeine, and we would both be giving up coffee. What next...red meat, jelly beans, horror flicks? Control is another nasty C word. I grabbed my toothbrush, left the tracksuit behind, and picked up a six-pack on my way home.

Kendra: I was excited when he invited me to his apartment for some naughty afternoon delight. I envisioned a chilled bottle of Chablis and a rose on the pillow. But what I got was a perfect view of the kitchen sink full of dirty dishes swimming in water that can be described as sewage and a bathroom with the ambiance of a service station men's room. Listen up, guys. An unflushed toilet is not conducive to foreplay!

Rhoda: I was introduced to a musician at a singles club and made a date to meet him the next afternoon at a sidewalk café downtown. The coffee was good, but our conversation was more monologue than dialogue. He was the only one talking. At one point, when he took a sip of his cappuccino, I seized the opportunity to squeeze in a little snippet about myself. His response was, "As I was saying…blah, blah, blah." When my coffee was finished, so was the date with that narcissist. I could tell he was the type who would constantly need his ego stroked. He could go stroke himself!

Cindy: The biggest boost to my self-esteem was when I dated a wonderful man who was shortsighted. Don was an author, and those thick lenses hid the most beautiful blue eyes. He never wore glasses in bed, so I always looked good naked to him. His lack of vision took away any inhibitions I had about my body, and I didn't even worry about the hail damage on my hips. I must confess—I even stooped to hiding his glasses so I could walk around in the buff. Then I'd feel guilty when I'd hear him crashing around the room trying to find them. But Bausch + Lomb put an end to all that bare freedom when Don discovered extended-wear contact lenses.

Connie: Glenn was a painter who thought foreplay was watching The Godfather trilogy in bed. Instead of finding a horse's head under the covers, I was afraid I'd wake up with the other end. The evening ended before the credits rolled.

Fran: I dated a firefighter who spent his downtime working out with state-of-the-art gym equipment while on duty. I was a busy, single working mom and kept our dates to weekends only, but he would call me daily. Each call started with his detailed description of the complete physical workout he had done that day—from top to bottom. After a few dates, I noticed whenever we encountered a person who had a few extra pounds, he would smirk and resort to childish whispered name calling. "Sit-up champ" was his favorite. I had no trouble staying trim due to my hectic schedule but wondered what his reaction would be if I gained weight. The first time I was invited to his house, he put on some crooning country music and spent a considerable amount of time attempting to light the fireplace. While he fumbled with the matches, I glanced through a photo album lying on the coffee table (well, it was more under the table…in a pile of newspapers). The album held some old pictures of him with his daughters when they were little—and he was big. He could have been a stand-in for the Stay Puft Marshmallow man. Those pictures showed me a man with double standards. I don't like double standards…and I don't like country music!

Corey: I had arranged to meet a blind date for dinner at a Boston Pizza near my office, after work. When I got to the restaurant, Charles was already seated with a couple of menus in front of him. After we'd placed our food order and the server had picked up the menus, I noticed several newspaper clippings on the table. My first thought was they had been left behind by the waitress or a previous patron, so I ignored them. Charles looked down and slid them across the table in front of me. One glance told me they were classified ads for swingers groups and sex toys. I balled them into my fist and threw them onto the floor. Good-Time Charlie picked them up, smoothed them on the table surface, and said, "Well… read them." I excused myself to go to the ladies' room and walked out the front door.

Marcie: Frank lived in a small rural community, and we maintained a long-distance relationship through social media for several months. He was perfect for me. I invited him to my place in the city for a weekend and bought a beautiful new duvet, with matching linens for the bed. When the doorbell rang, I greeted his familiar Facebook smile with open arms. His arms were empty, except for a battered backpack—no flowers, no candy, no wine. I wore a new silk shirt with the top buttons open, and he sported a pair of baggy, old sweatpants. As I showed him around the apartment, I realized those pants were a convenience to accommodate a rousing game of championship pocket pool he played throughout the tour. While I prepared lunch, he went to the bathroom and peed with the door open. Faint strains of dueling banjos played in my head. After we had finished eating, he leaned back with a loud belch, slapped his stomach, and winked at me. When the dishes were done, I sent Frank back to his rural roots. That village should not be deprived of its idiot.

Catherine: I think back to a disastrous date I had with a man who was destined to become one of my ex-husbands. He invited me to a formal corporate dinner, and I decided to utilize a little fashion trick I gleaned from the shop where I purchased my evening gown. We were the best-looking couple on the dance floor and ended the evening with a nightcap at my place. We all know what that means. I put a sheer red scarf over the lamp shade and proceeded to do a little striptease for him. But when I peeled off my new slinky dress, my future ex-husband recoiled from the sight. This was far from the reaction I had anticipated, so I ran to bathroom, where a quick glance in the mirror revealed the source of his shock. I had forgotten to remove the two Band-Aids I'd previously placed on my boobs under the backless top, in lieu of a bra. Thankfully, we were both able to laugh about it and bring our date to a satisfactory climax—er, conclusion.

Lucy: I met a great guy who was very good to me, but there was always that "thing" that just didn't seem right. We dated for a while and soon exchanged keys for weekend sleepovers. The arrangement worked well for me because he went back to his place during the week, and I had time to myself. At the end of the year, I looked forward to my annual business trip more than ever. Perhaps absence would make my heart grow fonder. But instead, I came home to a big surprise. He had sublet his condo, put his furniture in storage, and moved into my house! *What*...isn't that something couples discuss beforehand? I tried my best to make it work but couldn't. That "thing" was still there, and it had to go. It was him!

Clara: I was treating myself to a quiet Saturday afternoon at a small art gallery and noticed a neat-looking young gentleman, with Buddy Holly–style glasses, smiling at me. We introduced ourselves while moving through the exhibit and engaged in a pleasant and funny conversation regarding all things we didn't know about art. When we reached the last painting, Curt asked if I would like to meet him for coffee the next day. It's true. You can meet someone special when you're not looking!

I put on my favorite "best impression" outfit, but when I arrived at Finer Coffee, there was no sign of Curt. I ordered a latte and scone and waited at a table. After several minutes he walked in with a young woman holding a squalling baby. Curt introduced his wife and daughter and began to display an enormous amount of multilevel marketing material on the table in front of me. I stood up, pushed the literature to the floor, and threw some money on the table for my order.

"Shame on you!" My voice filled the room. "You led me to believe this was going to be a date!" I only have one regret about my actions: I shouldn't have left the money.

Kim: He talked about his ex-wife on our first date and all subsequent dates. I heard every single detail about her breathtaking beauty, her inspiring spirituality, and her fabulous fashion sense—right down to the cup size of her bra. When I told him I wasn't comfortable having her name mentioned in our conversations, he began referring to her as "the woman." He took her picture from his wallet at my office Christmas party and showed it to one of my coworkers. I put on my coat and left him to fondle the comfort blanket of his former marriage.

The next guy I dated differentiated between his two ex-wives by referring to them as "the slut" or "the bitch." I started looking for someone who'd never been married.

Izzy: I met Dan through an online-dating website, and he arranged for our initial meet and greet to be at McDonalds. He was really nice, but…hmm, probably could have found a better place than the golden arches for a first "date." We talked about where we worked and all the things you talk about when you first meet someone. The next day, he showed up at my office…wow! How nice of him to take time during his lunch break to visit me. I came down the stairs, excited to see him, and that really nice guy handed me two plastic sunflowers with tags from Dollarama still attached. Thanks for the gift, but no thanks for a future. I had already struggled through the wieners-and-beans years and had no interest in doing it again. This time, I wanted the flowers to be real.

Tammy: I thought I had met shades of a real-life Christian Grey. He had some interesting ideas on what he liked in the bedroom.

And, I must say, Grey's anatomy was well equipped for the job. At first I was intrigued...my very own Christian! As the weeks went by, his requests became increasingly strange and a bit weird, by my standards. He bought me a set of plastic handcuff earrings with matching necklace—cheap and nasty. When it comes to jewelry, diamonds are a girl's best friend. He also showed me some of his other purchases, strange-looking objects. I had no idea what they were or their intended use. When I saw something that looked like a plug...I said fifty kinds of *no*! It was too much of a gray area for me.

Guess Who's Coming to Dinner

Of the many dating stories I gathered from women for this book, I received the greatest number about dining experiences. An invitation to dinner is a common first or second date and is a good litmus test of compatibility. How is his dinner conversation? What are his eating habits and manners like? Does he scoop alfredo sauce from his chin with a fork or use a napkin? Is he quick to pick up the check, or does he leave it untouched to become the awkward elephant in the room, with its uncomfortable bulk on the table between you? If you offer to pitch in for the meal, does he refuse or calculate your share right down to the penny—plus tax?

I believe another important marker of a date's personality can be found in his treatment of people in the service industry. Is he cordial, rude, demanding? What kind of tip does he leave—too little, too much? In a group setting, does he volunteer to take all the cash to the till and pay the tab with his credit card? That little trick allows him to use any extra tip money to cover his portion of the bill. He gets a free meal, and the hard-working waitstaff end up with little or nothing for their efforts.

Another type of dinner date is a home-cooked meal. It can be more relaxing than eating in a restaurant and gives you a good opportunity to show him your home as well as your skills in the kitchen. If the budget is tight, good old home cooking is a great way to stretch it. Preparing food to share with someone can be an intimate act of care. If your date cooks for you, it's a good indication of how comfortable he is in the kitchen and how much of that you can expect in the future. Here are a few foodie stories the girls shared with me.

Claudette: I've never been a great cook, so perhaps it was a bit overambitious to invite a new boyfriend to have dinner with me and my family over the holidays. Joe arrived with wine and flowers but seemed unimpressed when I told him I'd neglected to take the turkey out of the freezer. And he showed a definite lack of enthusiasm at my announcement of our new traditional family dinner—Thanksgiving spaghetti Bolognese. He followed me into the kitchen to open the wine and screamed like a little girl when I broke the long pasta strands into the boiling water. The look on his face told me it was over for us when I brought out a half-gallon of Prego and the powdered Parmesan. Joe was Italian.

Sherry: Trent enjoyed every morsel of my famous catch-a-man beef Wellington but hurried out before I could serve dessert. As I cleared the dishes, I noticed my well-worn copy of *Get-Your-Man-to-Marry-You Plan* on the sideboard. No wonder he ran.

Melissa: "I can't even remember the last time a guy took me out on a date and actually paid for it." Those lyrics from Everclear's "Unemployed Boyfriend" seemed to be my mantra. I'd been on enough pizza and beer dates. I just wanted to be treated to a nice steak dinner while I still had all of my own teeth!

Emma: He invited me out to dinner and finished a huge porterhouse with an entire bottle of Cabernet sauvignon. I had the fettuccine alfredo, and because I was our chauffeur for the evening, I paired my meal with a lovely Colombian dark roast. When the check came, he asked me to pay half. He didn't get it, and that's not all he didn't get!

Lynn: Terry had renovated a beautiful old period home and promised to make his signature seafood chowder for me if I could fit some of his old curtains to the new windows. I lugged my sewing machine over to his place and spent the entire day altering drapery. By the time the window coverings were pressed and hanging in place, I was starving. We went to a local supermarket, and while my stomach growled, he spent a considerable amount of time sharing his vast knowledge of seafood while selecting a large quantity of expensive ingredients for the chowder. When we got to the checkout, he took his wallet out of his pants pocket but didn't open it. He turned to me and asked, "Do you want me to get this?" He was fortunate that my vocal cords were paralyzed by the shock of his request. The chowder was watery and bland—like him. I left the dishes in the sink and didn't go back for seconds—of anything!

Wanda: I had a wonderful dinner date with a handsome, interesting man and decided to keep in touch to see where that first date would take us. Chris didn't seem as interested in the convenience of modern communication as I was. Whenever I sent him a text, he would immediately pick up the phone and call me. In a world of instant messaging, I found it strange that someone would actually want to talk on the phone—so 1980s. When I asked him about it, he said he would much rather hear my voice than read my words. *Wow*—so 1980s romantic!

After three months of dating, we went on a weekend getaway. That's always a big test for a new relationship. The first night, while stumbling over those three little words, Chris whispered, "I want to die with you." My mind jumped to all kinds of crazy places. What does that mean, is he going to kill me—or both of us? The look on my face told him exactly what I was thinking, and he started to laugh. Chris explained that he wanted to spend the rest of his life with me, until the end. Whew, glad he made that clarification. Then I heard those three precious words: "I love you."

Less than a year after that first weekend getaway, we moved in together and started to share life as a couple. We soon established a special little ritual where we would take turns making breakfast on weekends. Christmas was two weeks away, and I was busy making a list of the million things I needed to do, while I waited for my Sunday breakfast. Chris was reading the paper—also waiting. It was a standoff. I finally gave in and grabbed the bacon and eggs from the fridge. When I opened the carton, there were only four eggs, and each one had a word on it printed in bold, black letters. WILL YOU MARRY ME? I turned to find Chris down on one knee, opening a tiny red velvet box with the most beautiful diamond ring inside. He's not rich and doesn't have big, fancy toys, but he holds my hand, kisses me every day, and is genuine, and he is truly my best friend. I'm a lucky girl!

9

THE BEST IS YET TO COME

Dear Friend,

We've traveled a long way together through the journey of my divorce, and I'm glad you stuck with me to the end. If you also soldiered bravely on to survive your own breakup battle, you will have experienced some victories and losses, just as I did. My income had increased, but so had my expenses. The kids were getting older and more independent, but they were asking to borrow the car. I was shopping for a house but couldn't afford the ones my realtor was showing me.

Shaken, Not Stirred

As with most Saturdays, Middle Child was spending the afternoon at his driver-education class, and Peewee was at band camp. Preparation for a backyard suntan session with my daughter was interrupted by incessant ringing. I couldn't ignore it. The telephone line was now the umbilical cord that connected me to my children.

"Hello."

I sensed a strange trepidation when I heard a soft male voice on the phone. "Hi, Linda. How are you doing?"

"Who is this?" My tone had a suspicious edge.

"It's me. Hub."

"Oh, sorry. I didn't recognize…" To laugh or not to laugh, that was the dilemma. I laughed.

Hub was not amused and launched into a jumbled rant about what a sad state of affairs his life had become. "Came home… found wife in bed with best friend…packed bags…drinking alone every night…let's go out for dinner, and who knows…"

It had been a long time since I'd been out for a nice meal, and I had no plans that evening. For a moment, I was shaken by my fragile loneliness, but, as Hub continued with his pathetic tale of woe, I began to feel a bizarre detachment. I interrupted. "Dinner sounds nice, Hub, but what you're really saying is that you got kicked in the sack, and now you want me to put ice on it."

"Well, no. I mean, yeah…I mean…"

"No, thanks. I'm worth more than a rebound dinner and your hopes for pity sex."

The Frog Prince

The testosterone-related skepticism that had kept me single reared again when Jennifer stopped by my office one Friday afternoon to set me up on a blind date.

"Syd works for the railroad and dabbles in electronics. He's installing the sound system at my studio and would be perfect for you!" Jennifer grinned like a Cheshire cat.

"What's the catch—ugly, married, serial killer?"

Jennifer assured me Syd was none of those things and offered an additional, albeit confusing, testimonial. "He used to be a Brit, but he isn't anymore."

"Look, I don't care what country he's from. I've been fighting a cold all week and just want to go home and crawl into my old chair."

"You'll be fine. You can order the chicken soup. He's promised me a steak dinner if I can get him a date, so I'm coming with you."

"Hmm...sounds a bit pimpish to me."

"All is fair in love and war, and judging by how few dates you've had recently, you need an ally in the battle."

Jennifer picked me up at seven, and we drove to Syd's neat little bungalow for a predinner cocktail. Any apprehension I had dissolved in his warm handshake and wonderful smile. He was dressed to impress in a three-piece suit and tie, and it worked. A quick glance at the décor of his home told me Syd was still very much a Brit, so I asked for a sherry. That was to impress him. A sign above the door to his man cave read, "In here, don't even think about football, hockey, or country music!" I was beginning to like this man more every minute, and, with that dreamy English accent, he could make a fart joke sound in good taste.

Even his restaurant choice couldn't spoil the evening. It was good to be back at the Red Carpet. Dinner was a pleasure—no awkward moments and no lack of conversation. When we had finished dessert, Jennifer excused herself to attend to an ailing goldfish, and Syd took me to a little British pub for a nightcap. Now what? Do I like him enough to go out with him again? Will he ask me? Should I ask him? It was time for a test.

After watching Hub lose his sense of humor over the course of our marriage, it was important for me to have someone to share a laugh with. If people can't see a funny side to life, they don't look at life the way I do. So I told a joke. It was a bit naughty...okay, it was dirty. A relationship-make-or-break type of joke. I held my breath and watched that warm smile widen into a wonderful, hearty laugh.

For our second date, Syd took me to an Italian restaurant with white linen and the best pasta I've ever had. After dinner, he told me he had rented a Lethal Weapon movie for us to watch because all women love Mel Gibson. To me that meant he was secure in his masculinity, but I didn't tell him I wasn't one to swoon over Mel.

We spent the next three or four dates packing for my move to a duplex I had just bought. It was small but was the first place I'd owned without a man's name on the title. That would have been a perfect time for a lesser man to cut and run, but Syd hung in there. He was a tremendous help and even cleaned the old Birch Street house after we had moved out.

Syd completely won my heart with little things. He cooked dinner often, he washed his hands after using the bathroom, and he put the cap back on the toothpaste. The first time I stayed overnight at his place, he showed me some special purchases he'd made for me at Bath & Body Works, so I modeled the ones I'd picked up for him at La Senza.

How Many Boyfriends Does It Take to Change a Lightbulb?
After the kids and I were settled into our duplex, I noticed a few things I had missed before the purchase. All the light switches were upside down, two burners on the stove didn't work, milk soured in the fridge, and ice cream wouldn't stay frozen in the freezer. Our housewarming bucket of Cherry Garcia was served for breakfast, lunch, and dinner.

Syd was spending his Saturdays at my house with his toolbox in exchange for home-cooked meals. After the ill-fated chicken tartare incident, I realized the oven didn't heat above 250 degrees. Thankfully no one got sick, and Syd still came back the following weekend with tools. By then, I had claimed the little warren at the end of the hall as my office and set to work organizing it while he worked on a clogged sink in the adjacent bathroom. The only thing he'd been tasked with that day was to fix the shower door so I could get rid of the perverted plastic curtain. It had a creepy way of brushing up against me like a lecherous old uncle at a family reunion. Although Syd's focus was supposed to be on the offending shower curtain, he had noticed the bathroom sink was draining slower than his standards would allow, so he decided to tackle that instead.

When I'd finished setting up the office, I moved to the dining room to hang Jennifer's beautiful housewarming gift—a framed collage of the family photos she had taken at the music festival. I was curious on how Syd's job was coming along when I heard language from the worksite increase substantially in volume, as well as irreverence. Investigation revealed he had stabbed a hole through the antiquated bathroom drainpipe with a wire coat hanger.

At last, peace fell upon the house. Syd had left on a supply run to the hardware store. Was this the calm before the storm? I took the opportunity to have a quiet cup of coffee and a quick thumb through the Yellow Pages for a plumber. I also wondered about the project's final price tag. In my experience, DIY could be expensive. First came the cost of supplies, then the occasional outlay for a professional to finish the job, and finally the price of treating me to dinner to get away from the mess. But to my surprise, the pipe was fixed without further mishap.

Invigorated by the success of the drain repair, Syd moved on to the next challenge: changing a lightbulb in the kitchen. This project was in full view from the dining room. I kept my eyes on my work as he reached up to the little television on top of the fridge and turned to his favorite show, *The Borgias*. The infamous fifteenth-century pope and his felonious family burst onto the screen and into my concentration. Syd and I differed on the definition of that miniseries. He called it a period drama. I called it medieval porn. I'm no prude, but I had to wonder how much of the bedchamber rumpy-pumpy was historical fact or just good for ratings.

I began to gather tools to move away from the blaring Borgias when Syd climbed up on the stepstool and began to loosen the cover of the kitchen light fixture. A metallic click of the tiny screw resounded through the room as it slipped through his fingers and bounced onto the floor. Even the wall clock seemed to hush as the screw rolled merrily along and out of sight underneath the refrigerator. Syd jumped off the stool and began to wrench the fridge from its snug fit in the kitchen alcove.

I decided an offer of assistance would likely offend his masculinity, so I pretended not to watch the proceedings as they played out in front of me. As Syd continued to move the appliance out from its place, I snuck a quick peek in time to see the TV's electrical cord reach its full length and drag the little Sony off the back of the fridge. It crashed against the wall and dangled near the floor, still attached by the cord, swaying to and fro like some kind of babbling, bungee-jumping Borgia.

Now girls, you know how important a good laugh is to me, but I realized that would have been inappropriate. I kept my head down on an invisible task, but my eyes were on the show in the kitchen. An irate Syd reached down and yanked the cord up out of its socket with such force the TV became airborne and clipped the wall clock on its upward flight. The electronic duo sailed through the air in a slow-motion movie scene and landed in a shattered heap on the floor.

Laughter bubbled under my surface, but suppression was the only option. I remained silent as Syd swept up the various bits of small appliance and moved the fridge back into place. Only then did he realize he hadn't retrieved the tiny screw from its new home with the refrigerator dust bunnies. Refusing to tackle the monster Frigidaire again, he set about rooting through a jumble of nuts and bolts in his toolbox for a substitute. To my great amazement, a replacement screw was found in short order, and the bulb was replaced and the light-fixture cover secured in place. Syd climbed off the stool and stepped back to survey his handiwork with smug satisfaction. Then, as he bent to pick up his tools, the light cover came crashing down beside his head.

We both laughed! This time dinner was on me.

Diary of a Country Bumpkin

The three words most likely to strike fear in my heart have always been "meet my mother." With Syd's mother across the pond in England, I felt safe from any worries about that. We had been dating for almost six months when Syd surprised me with another three words: tickets to London!

To compound my mother-in-law phobia was the fact that it would be my first time abroad. I grew up in a rural setting, and my traveling experience was mostly for business and a ghastly Yellowstone vacation with Hub years ago. Syd reassured me that England had been his home for many years, and he would be my personal tour guide. There would be no language barrier, and money conversion was simple. By departure date, I was packed and ready. Careful planning ensured I had everything I needed, including sufficient pounds sterling.

Syd had briefed me on some of the wonderful culture and habits of the British, and, as a woman, I took special note of one important fact—public washrooms. I learned they could be referred to as many different things—the loo, the bog, WC, or, most often, simply the toilet. After the long wait to deplane at Heathrow and get through customs, I was relieved to see the universal sign of a women's washroom over a doorway down the hall. I dashed in but was stopped by coin slots on all the doors. I had currency notes with me but no change. Thankfully, another traveler took pity at the sight of my panic-stricken face and fronted me twenty pence.

When I questioned Syd on why I hadn't been told that small detail, he shrugged and said, "Blokes don't need coin for the lav."

That rocky start to the holiday was soon forgotten in the profound beauty of the English villages and lush countryside. Syd's mother was lovely and welcoming, and I got caught up in the history surrounding us: Hadrian's Wall, Stonehenge, the castles and cathedrals. I was struck by was how narrow the streets and sidewalks were, compared to the vastness of Canada. We saw a family of four cycling merrily down a narrow lane with vehicles zooming by at high speeds. I thought it would have been safer for them to add chainmail to the helmets.

I was completely enamored by the quaint country and its quirks. Horses and riders frequented village amenities, and dogs were allowed everywhere—in shops, pubs, and even on buses and trains. When we visited the ancient Roman city of Bath, I was hooked for life. I had several hours to browse through the many antique shops on my own, while Syd scouted jewelry stores for his passion: clocks and timepieces. I was given a speedy education on the lack of pedestrian right of way by a large garbage truck, or bin lorry, that ran me off the road.

Late afternoon, I met Syd in the market square at our pre-arranged time, and we sat on a bench comparing our acquired treasures. I had purchased an antique garnet brooch, a Shetland sheep throw rug, a Royal Albert China figurine, and a handmade Swaledale sweater. Syd bought a watch.

Tea had been plentiful that afternoon, but public washrooms were few and far between. I looked around and spotted a large red sign in a third-floor window, high above a small tea shop. *TOILET.*

"I can't go all the way up there to the bathroom. I'll never make it!" I grabbed Syd's arm and pointed to the sign.

"No, love, it says 'TO LET'—that's a vacant flat."

Happily Ever After

There have been more wonderful trips to England for Syd and me during the years that followed. Unfortunately, we each brought our own set of baggage into the relationship and not just the ones used for travel. Syd recognized early on that it was of paramount importance for me to maintain the independence I had once lost, and he has allowed me to have that. I assured him of my sincere loyalty, since he struggled with trust issues from previous betrayals. We have both worked hard to put past experiences behind us and build a solid future together. I can honestly say we are as comfortable with each other as a pair of relaxed-fit denims and orthotics.

We take in sci-fi movies with the understanding that I might slip out to a theater next door to watch another show. He doesn't mind if I finish all the Pringles when he's not looking, and I know he sometimes wipes his shoes with my tea towels. We respect each other as individuals, as well as equals, and have never lost sight of the funny side of life. The couple who laughs, lasts!

Linda Penner learned how much a sense of humor, and a funny book, can help to get through the dark days of divorce. With first-hand experience at the trials of being a single mother and career woman, she vowed to channel her own life experiences into a laugh-out-loud examination of the aftereffects of divorce in support of other women going through similar crises.

Penner is an accomplished writer. She became passionate about writing and storytelling as a young child, took college literary programs, and is currently in a writer's club. Her work has been published in *Canadian Stories Magazine* and *The LifeStory Institute*.

Penner spent her career in the financial industry. She now lives a charmed life of retirement in southern Alberta, Canada with her dog, Beau, and Syd, her stalwart and true Frog Prince.

78974262R00090

Made in the USA
Columbia, SC
22 October 2017